Film, TV and Music

Multi-level photocopiable activities for teenagers

Olha Madylus

CAMBRIDGE
UNIVERSITY PRESS

CAMBRIDGE UNIVERSITY PRESS
Cambridge, New York, Melbourne, Madrid, Cape Town, Singapore,
São Paulo, Delhi, Dubai, Tokyo

Cambridge University Press
The Edinburgh Building, Cambridge CB2 8RU, UK

www.cambridge.org
Information on this title: www.cambridge.org/9780521728386

First published 2009
Reprinted 2010

Designed and produced by Kamae Design, Oxford

Printed in China by Sheck Wah Tong Printing Press Limited

A catalogue record for this publication is available from the British Library

ISBN 978-0-52172838-6

Contents

Map of the book

 **1 Film**

Title	Level	Language focus	Skills focus	Activity type
1.1 Matching pairs	Elementary	vocabulary of types of film	vocabulary building	a matching game
1.2 What films do you like?	Elementary	asking and answering questions in the present simple	speaking and listening	a questionnaire
1.3 My superhero	Elementary	giving and asking for personal information in the present simple	speaking and writing	a mingle interviewing activity
1.4 The real Harry Potter	Elementary	reading about personal information	reading and writing	sentence matching
1.5 What happens next?	Elementary	writing a storyboard	reading, writing and speaking	creating a storyboard
2.1 Can you picture it?	Intermediate	reading descriptive language	reading	drawing a character based on a written description
2.2 Little monsters	Intermediate	descriptive vocabulary	writing and listening	writing a description then listening to a description and producing a drawing
2.3 Film crossword	Intermediate	general film vocabulary	vocabulary building	a crossword
2.4 Which film?	Intermediate	writing film blurbs	reading and writing	a matching activity, then writing film blurbs
2.5 Say it with feeling!	Intermediate	language used in films	speaking and intonation	a board game
2.6 Title, character, action	Intermediate	talking about films	speaking and writing	a speaking card game
3.1 Scary or weird?	Upper intermediate	reading about film genres	reading and speaking	a jigsaw reading
3.2 Do you agree?	Upper intermediate	agreeing and disagreeing	speaking	a discussion game
3.3 Crazy film plots	Upper intermediate	relative clauses	writing and speaking	a sentence-creation game
3.4 Stars in their eyes	Upper intermediate	reading a biography	reading and speaking	a jigsaw reading
3.5 I haven't a clue	Upper intermediate	writing definitions	writing and speaking	a pair crossword

Map of the book

2 TV

Title	Level	Language focus	Skills focus	Activity type
1.1 People and programmes	Elementary	vocabulary of TV programmes and people	vocabulary building and writing	a matching game
1.2 Is it on every day?	Elementary	asking and answering present tense questions	speaking	a guessing game
1.3 Give me a clue!	Elementary	vocabulary of TV programmes and people	writing clues	a pair crossword
1.4 The weakest link	Elementary	present simple questions; superlatives	speaking and listening	role playing a TV quiz game
1.5 Silent TV	Elementary	vocabulary of TV programmes	reading	a mime game
1.6 Talk, talk, talk!	Elementary	talking about habits and likes and dislikes	speaking	a board game
2.1 What shall we watch?	Intermediate	reading for key information; negotiating	reading and speaking	a negotiating game
2.2 Guess what I watch!	Intermediate	asking and answering questions using different tenses	speaking	a guessing game and mingle activity
2.3 And now, here is the news ...	Intermediate	news headlines and stories using the present perfect and past simple	reading, writing and speaking	a matching game, then completing news reports and presenting the news
2.4 Design a game show	Intermediate	modal verbs for rules	reading and speaking	reading the rules of game shows, then designing a new game show
2.5 Commercial break	Intermediate	the language of advertising; comparatives, superlatives and intensifiers	reading and speaking	a matching game, then creating a TV commercial
3.1 Who's who in the soap?	Upper intermediate	describing people and talking about personal information	reading for detail	an information-seeking game
3.2 How much do you know about TV?	Upper intermediate	discussing facts about TV; agreeing and disagreeing; the passive	reading and speaking	a discussion game
3.3 TV snakes and ladders	Upper intermediate	expressing opinions	speaking	a discussion board game
3.4 Is TV bad for children?	Upper intermediate	discussing advantages and disadvantages	reading and speaking	a role-play discussion
3.5 What happens next?	Upper intermediate	creating a TV drama plot	speaking	group creation of a drama plot based on picture prompts

Map of the book

3 Music

Title	Level	Language focus	Skills focus	Activity type
1.1 Musical pairs	Elementary	vocabulary of musical instruments; asking and answering questions in the present simple	speaking	a matching game then a mingle activity
1.2 Interview with a star	Elementary	asking and answering personal questions in the present simple and past simple	reading and speaking	a matching task, then a role-play interview
1.3 My song	Elementary	pronunciation and rhyming words	listening and writing	a pronunciation maze, then completing song lyrics
1.4 A musical survey	Elementary	using quantifiers and talking about graphs	speaking	conducting a survey, presenting the findings as a graph, then talking about the graph
1.5 Musical record breakers	Elementary	asking and answering questions in the present simple, past simple and present perfect	reading for specific information and speaking	a jigsaw reading and role-play interview
1.6 Musical fashions	Elementary	describing people	speaking and listening	vocabulary matching, then a picture dictation
2.1 Music crossword	Intermediate	writing definitions of general music vocabulary	speaking and listening	a pair crossword
2.2 Interview with a star	Intermediate	asking and answering questions about a career in music	writing and speaking	preparing and acting out a role-play interview
2.3 Beat the clock!	Intermediate	talking and giving opinions about music	speaking	a speaking game
2.4 Hip hop quiz	Intermediate	vocabulary of music and music culture	reading	a quiz, including information-gathering
2.5 An overnight success	Intermediate	discussing options and making decisions	reading and speaking	a reading maze with group discussion
3.1 Boy band or heavy metal?	Upper intermediate	reading descriptions of different types of bands	reading and speaking	a jigsaw reading and discussion
3.2 Music spiral	Upper intermediate	expressing ideas and opinions about music	speaking	a speaking game
3.3 Song lyrics	Upper intermediate	rhyme, rhythm, stress and intonation	reading and writing	reading and writing song lyrics
3.4 Musical jobs	Upper intermediate	writing a job advert and job application	reading and writing	writing job adverts, writing applications, then role playing interviews
3.5 The big event	Upper intermediate	negotiating and planning a music event	speaking	a group negotiating activity

Introduction

What is *Film, TV and Music*?

Film, TV and Music is a photocopiable resource book designed to give teenage students the opportunity to practise language in meaningful and enjoyable ways. Each activity has been designed to appeal particularly to teenagers, and to be multiply intelligent, so that teenagers can use their own particular strengths to help with their language learning. The activities are also designed to be fun. All teachers know that it can sometimes be difficult to motivate students, but if students enjoy the activities they are involved in during their English lessons, they will find it much easier to participate and learn.

Who is *Film, TV and Music* for?

Film, TV and Music is for teachers of English whose students are aged from 11–16, and who want to use activities on topics that will interest and engage teenagers. This book can be used to supplement any course-book material or to provide self-contained lessons. The activity sheets are clear and simple to use, with minimal preparation required.

How is *Film, TV and Music* organised?

Film, TV and Music is divided into three sections, each covering one broad topic area. Within each section, units are subdivided into three levels: elementary, intermediate and upper intermediate.

The map of the book and the focus boxes at the start of each activity give information about which lexical, grammatical and skill areas are covered. With each activity, step-by-step instructions are given, as well as an indication of how much preparation and class time the activity should take.

What type of activities are there in *Film, TV and Music*?

Film, TV and Music includes a wide variety of activity types, from jigsaw readings, quizzes and surveys to crosswords and board games. Wherever possible, students are encouraged to be creative and express themselves through their work. In the follow-up activities, they are also encouraged to focus on their own particular areas of interest.

What skills are practised in the activities?

In *Film, TV and Music* there is plenty of practice of all the language skills – reading, writing, listening and speaking. Students will also be able to practise familiar grammar through fun activities, and extend and develop their vocabulary through topics that interest them. Although many activities have one particular language focus, most of the activities also provide a variety of challenges, incorporating several different skills or grammar topics.

What are multiple intelligences?

Howard Gardner's theory of multiple intelligences suggests that different individuals are intelligent in different ways (Howard Gardner, *Frames of Mind: The Theory of Multiple Intelligences*). Gardner identifies seven different types of intelligence:
Linguistic – reading, writing, story-telling, debating, word puzzles
Mathematical – reasoning, logic, problem-solving, discovering patterns
Visual/Spatial – maps, charts, mazes, visualisation
Kinaesthetic – movement, dancing, drama, crafts
Musical – songs, rhythms, phonology
Interpersonal – working in groups, sharing, communicating
Intrapersonal – working alone, reflection

How does *Film, TV and Music* use the theory of multiple intelligences?

The activities in *Film, TV and Music* are designed to tap into the different types of intelligences, so that individual students can bring their own personal strengths to their language learning. The main activities are designed to incorporate several different intelligences and styles of learning, and in many of the follow-up activities several different possibilities are suggested, from giving presentations to producing posters, so that students can choose an activity that appeals to their individual style of learning. In this way, all students will gain a sense of achievement from the activities.

How does *Film, TV and Music* encourage motivation?

The activities in *Film, TV and Music* are designed to reflect the fact that individual students have their own particular hobbies and areas of interest. Follow-up activities encourage students to pursue these interests, for example by searching websites for information on their favourite television programme or giving a presentation on a style of music that appeals to them. By tapping into students' natural enthusiasm, the activities will motivate students and make their learning meaningful to them.

How does *Film, TV and Music* help give students a sense of pride and achievement?

Film, TV and Music uses a portfolio approach to learning. Students are encouraged to produce creative work which they can keep and share with others. This gives students tangible evidence of their progress, and helps them to celebrate their learning and take pride in their achievements. Encourage your students to keep a portfolio of their work in a loose-leaf folder, which they can add to as they complete each activity. They can use their portfolio to monitor their own progress, and can also show it to friends and parents and look back on it later with a sense of achievement.

How is each activity organised?

Each activity offers the teacher a warm-up task to lead in to the main activity, and several suggestions for follow-up activities. The main activity is explained clearly and simply and will guide you through the stages of the lesson. The follow-up activities are designed to allow students to develop the ideas and language from the main activities in a creative or personalised way, to encourage students' motivation and engagement with the learning process. The teaching notes are intended as a lesson plan. However, as with any lesson plan in any teacher's book, do adapt the activities to your students and to best suit your own teaching style and context.

An explanation of some key concepts in the teaching notes

Eliciting is a good way to start any lesson. It involves drawing out what students already know, and so gives a sense of achievement and engages them in the learning process. Discussing a subject before students begin an activity will activate their opinions, feelings and experiences on the subject and make the topic more accessible.

Brainstorming is one way of eliciting what students know, by encouraging students to write down or call out as many words and ideas relevant to a particular topic as possible, usually within a set time limit.

Research is important as it allows students to find out information on their own and so take responsibility for their own learning, increasing student autonomy. It also allows them to develop their own personal interests. Many of the follow-up activities involve an element of individual research.

Thanks and acknowledgements

The author would like to thank the following people: Claire Powell of Cambridge University Press for her hard work and generosity with ideas whilst working on this project, and Sheila Dignen, for her careful and creative editorial eye.

Many thanks to Merryn Grimley, Alena Literova, Maria de los Angeles Vélez Guzmán and Gillian Davidson for taking the time to review and pilot materials, providing invaluable feedback. Their help was vital in the development stages of *Film, TV* and *Music*.

The publishers are grateful for for permission to reproduce photographic material:

Alamy/Bluefly p111 (c), Alamy/Roger Cracknell OI/Classic p111 (tr); BBC Photo Library p87 (tr); Corbis/Eric Fougere/VIP Images p87 (tl); Getty Images p87 (c), Getty Images/Dimitrios Kambouris p17, Getty Images/Jo Hale p111 (br); Kobal Collection/20th Century Fox p27 (1,3,4,5) Kobal Collection/Eon/Danaq/UIP p27 (7), Kobal Collection/First National p27 (2), Kobal Collection/RKO p27 (8), Kobal Collection/Walt Disney Pictures p27 (6); Rex Features/NBCU Photobank p51.

The publishers are also grateful to the following artists:

Tony Forbes pp15, 23; Dylan Gibson pp11, 13, 25, 45, 63, 89, 102, 103; Kamae Design pp17, 35, 47, 55, 73, 85, 105; Mark Watkinson pp67, 77, 79, 93; Ned Woodman pp19, 65, 97.

The publishers are also grateful to the following contributors:

Sheila Dignen: Editorial work

Kamae Design Ltd: Text design, layouts and some images

Matching pairs

Language focus
vocabulary of types of film

Key vocabulary
types of film: *action film, comedy, cowboy film, horror film, love film, science fiction film, spy film, war film*

Skills focus
vocabulary building

Multiple intelligences
visual, linguistic and interpersonal

Level
elementary

Time
30 minutes

Preparation
one photocopy, cut up into cards, for each group of 3 or 4 students. The cards should be photocopied or stuck onto card if possible.

Extra notes
This kind of activity can be stored in the classroom and if you have early finishers in other lessons, they can play the game again and get some useful revision.

Warm-up

❶ Ask students if they like watching films.

❷ Elicit any English words students know to do with films and write them on the board. Encourage them to offer any word in English, even names of actors or films, to build their confidence.

❸ Ask students what their favourite type of film is, for example action films or films about love.

Main activity

❶ Put students into groups of three or four, and explain that they are going to play a game.

❷ Hand out a set of cards to each group and explain that the words on the cards all refer to types of films. Ask students to try to match the pictures to the names of the types of films. If you like, you could allow students to use dictionaries for this task.

❸ Check the answers to the matching task with the class (see the layout on the activity sheet for answers). Point out that most of the words for film types are compound nouns, e.g. *war film, horror film*, but *comedy* and *cartoon* are single words.

❹ Drill the words, so that students can hear them and say them.

❺ Ask the students to turn the cards over and jumble them up, then spread them out so they are lying on their desk face down.

❻ To demonstrate the game, ask one student to turn over two cards. As they do this, they should say the word they see, or the word that describes the picture they see. Explain that if the student turns over a word and picture that match, they can keep the cards. If the cards do not match, the student must turn the cards back over and it is the turn of the next student. Students continue taking turns to try to remember where the cards are and find matching pairs, until there are no cards left on the table. The winner is the student with the most matching pairs.

❼ While the groups are playing the game, walk round and monitor, checking for accurate pronunciation.

❽ Students can play the game a few times to help them memorise the new vocabulary.

Follow-up

○ Ask students to work in their groups and make lists of films they have seen under the headings of the film types. For example: Cartoons: *Finding Nemo, Ratatouille.*

○ Get students to compare their lists with other groups.

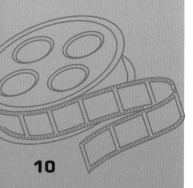

War film	Horror film	Cowboy film

Spy film	Love film	Science fiction film

Cartoon	Action film	Comedy

What films do you like?

Language focus
asking and answering questions in the present simple

Key vocabulary
types of film; *favourite*

Skills focus
speaking and listening

Multiple intelligences
linguistic, interpersonal and kinaesthetic

Level
elementary

Time
30 minutes

Preparation
one photocopy for each student

Extra notes
You could do activity Film 1.1 before you do this activity, to present the key vocabulary.

Warm-up

❶ Ask the students to guess what films you like. They may have some interesting ideas.

❷ Suggest that they might like to ask you what types of films you like, and elicit a few questions they could use. For example:
Do you like horror films?
Do you like comedies?
Do you like cartoons?

❸ Drill a few of the questions.

❹ Introduce the question: *What's your favourite horror film/war film etc.?*

❺ Invite different students to ask you the questions, and give your answers.

Main activity

❶ Give each student an activity sheet. Ask students to match the pictures to the film types. Check answers, and make sure students understand all the film types.

> **Answers**
> 1 war films   2 horror films   3 comedies   4 spy films   5 cartoons
> 6 action films   7 science fiction films   8 cowboy films   9 love films

❷ Explain to students that they are going to ask other students what types of films they like, and what their favourite films are. Model the activity with one student. Ask the questions, and show the students how to fill in the questionnaire.

❸ Tell students to go around the class and interview each other, filling in the sheet until it is full or until time runs out. You might like to set a time limit of ten minutes for the activity, to make sure it doesn't drag.

❹ Write these sentence frames on the board. Then ask students to stand up one at a time and report their findings.

_____ *likes* _____ *films. Her/his favourite is* _____.
_____ *doesn't like* _____ *films.*

Follow-up

○ Ask students to make a poster about the films they like, and tell them to include some of the sentences they have used in this activity. For example: *I like science fiction films. My favourite films are The Matrix and Star Wars.* They can draw pictures of the films or find pictures in magazines or on the internet to decorate their posters. This would be a nice homework task.

○ Alternatively, students could work in pairs or small groups and produce posters together in class.

○ These posters could be pinned up around the classroom to help remind students of the target language.

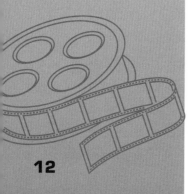

Name:	horror films	comedies	war films	cowboy films	cartoons	spy films	science fiction films	love films	action films
e.g. Anna	Yes, Frankenstein.	No.	No.	No.	Yes, Ratatouille.	Yes, James Bond.	No.	No.	Yes, Indiana Jones.

Film 1.3

My superhero

Language focus
giving and asking for personal information in the present simple

Key vocabulary
alias, costume, cover job, super powers

Skills focus
speaking and writing

Multiple intelligences
visual, linguistic, intrapersonal and interpersonal

Level
elementary

Time
40 minutes

Preparation
one photocopy, cut into Parts A and B, for each student

Warm-up

❶ Write the word SUPERHERO on the board and elicit the meaning.

❷ Put students into small groups and tell them they have two minutes to write down as many superheroes from films and cartoons as they can in English, for example: *Superman, Batman, Spiderman, X-men, Transformers.*

❸ Ask students what they know about Superman. Elicit that he has an *alias* (Clark Kent), and a *cover job* (he's a reporter).

Main activity

❶ Give each student Part A of the activity sheet. Go through it as a class and make sure that students understand what they have to do. Tell them to work individually and create their superhero identities. Tell them not to show other students.

❷ When students have finished, explain that they are going to ask each other about their identities, and then choose the best superhero.

❸ Elicit the questions that students will need to ask each other:
What's your name?
Where do you live?
What's your alias?
What cover job do you do?
What do you wear?
What can you do?

❹ Tell students to stand up and move around the class asking as many people as possible about themselves.

❺ Get feedback on which superhero identities students found funniest or best.

❻ Elicit some more 'super' names, aliases, costumes and super powers from the students, which they think are appropriate for a film hero(ine). Write some of these up on the board.

❼ Hand out Part B and ask students to write a description of a superhero and draw a picture. Tell them they can use a real film superhero, the one they used for this activity or a new one.

❽ Pin up these descriptions of the superheroes around the classroom. Ask students to look at all the superheroes and decide which ones they like the most. You could have a vote for best name, best powers etc.

Follow-up

○ Ask one student to come to the front of the class. Tell that student to think of a film superhero, but not say the name. Other students must guess the superhero by asking Yes/No questions such as *Can you fly?*

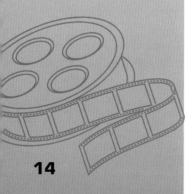

A

I am a superhero!

1 Choose the name of an animal, bird or insect.

My name is _____ boy/girl.

2 Think of a country which begins with the same letter as your name.

I live in _____.

3 Think of a) a first name, and b) the name of a fruit or vegetable.

My alias is _____ _____.

4 Think of a very boring job.

My cover job is a _____.

5 Think of two pieces of clothing and two colours.

I wear _____ _____ and _____ _____.

6 Think of two impossible things you would like to do.

I can _____ and _____.

B

My superhero

The real Harry Potter

Language focus
reading about personal information

Key vocabulary
colour, favourite, number, parents, pets, sport, star, was born

Skills focus
reading and writing

Multiple intelligences
linguistic and mathematical

Level
elementary

Time
45 minutes

Preparation
one photocopy, cut into parts A and B, for each pair of students

Extra notes
There is a variety of structures here that students would generally cover in an elementary-level course book. Therefore, this activity would be appropriate at the end of the elementary level. It could also be used at pre-intermediate level for revision.

Warm-up

❶ Ask students who their favourite film stars are.

❷ Ask what kind of information they like to know about their favourite film stars. Collect some key ideas on the board, for example: *age, brothers and sisters, pets, favourite music*, etc.

❸ Explain to students that they are going to read about Daniel Radcliffe, the actor who plays Harry Potter. Ask them if they know, or can guess, any of this personal information about him.

Main activity

❶ Put students into pairs and give each pair Part A of the activity sheet. Ask students to read the sentence beginnings and guess how the sentences end. Allow students to ask questions and look up words in their dictionaries to ensure they understand the language they encounter.

❷ Hand out Part B and ask the students to match the endings of the sentences with the beginnings.

❸ Check answers and ask students if they had guessed correctly.

> **Answers**
> 1 G   2 O   3 M   4 I   5 L   6 H   7 F   8 B   9 C   10 K   11 A   12 J   13 E   14 D   15 N

❹ Ask the students to read out the sentences round the class and check pronunciation.

Follow-up

○ Ask students to look at the sentences again and write similar sentences about their favourite actor. Students could do this for homework so that they can do research and find the information they need.

○ They can then read out their sentences to the class, and their classmates have to guess who they are describing.

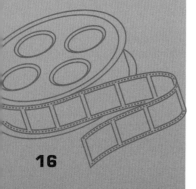

A

1 Daniel Radcliffe was born on...
2 He was born in...
3 He doesn't have any...
4 His parents are called...
5 His pets are...
6 He is the star of...
7 He has blue...
8 His favourite actors are...
9 He can play the...
10 His favourite number is...
11 His favourite colour is...
12 His favourite sport is...
13 He likes drinking...
14 He drives...
15 He likes watching...

B

A green.
B Cameron Diaz, Julia Roberts and Ben Stiller.
C bass guitar.
D a Fiat Punto.
E diet coke.
F eyes.
G 23 July 1989.
H the Harry Potter films.
I Alan and Marcia.
J football.
K nine.
L two dogs.
M brothers or sisters.
N 'The Simpsons'.
O London, England.

Film 1.5

What happens next?

Language focus
writing a storyboard

Key vocabulary
alien, careful, chase, crew, fantastic, land (v), peace, run away, shoot, spacecraft, storyboard, weapons

Skills focus
reading, writing and speaking

Multiple intelligences
visual, linguistic and kinaesthetic

Level
elementary

Time
45 minutes

Preparation
one photocopy, cut into parts A, B and C, for each group of 3 or 4 students. You will also need scissors, glue and a large sheet of paper or card for each group.

Extra notes
The follow-up activities could be done in the next lesson, especially if the students are enjoying creating their own film plots.

Warm-up

1 Tell the students to all stand up. Say: *We're going to make a film. What do we need?*

2 As students call out words, for example *actors*, clap your hands, say the word (e.g. *actors*) clearly and get all the students to repeat the word. The student(s) who called out that word then sit down.

3 Keep going until all the class is seated or they can think of no more words.

4 Write any new vocabulary on the board.

5 If nobody calls out *storyboard*, say that they have forgotten something really important and introduce the word. Explain that a storyboard contains pictures of each scene in a film, with some dialogue and instructions for the director.

Main activity

1 Put students into groups of three or four and give each group a copy of Part A of the activity sheet. Also give out scissors, glue and the large sheets of paper or card. Explain that the pictures form part of the storyboard of a film. Tell students to cut out the five pictures and arrange (but not glue) them in a logical order. Explain that there is no right and wrong answer to this activity, but students can use their own ideas. Encourage them to discuss where each picture should go. Explain that they will get more information later to help them create their story.

2 When students are happy with the order of their pictures, give out Part B. Tell students to cut out the speech bubbles and add them to their storyboard. Tell them they may want to change the order of the pictures to accommodate the speech bubbles.

3 When students are happy with their storyboards, hand out Part C. Explain that these are the film directions. Tell students to cut these out and add them to their storyboards. Again, they may want to change the order of the pictures and speech bubbles to accommodate the directions.

4 Once they are happy with their storyboard, they can glue it in place on their sheet of paper or card.

Follow-up

○ Ask groups to continue the storyboard for at least another five frames – drawing the pictures, adding speech or thought bubbles and directions. This could be done in a later lesson.

○ Students can either display their work around the class in order to look at each other's storyboards, or they could act out their scenes for each other.

○ Alternatively, working in groups of three or four, students could create their own storyboard. This could be based on a film they know, or they can use their imagination.

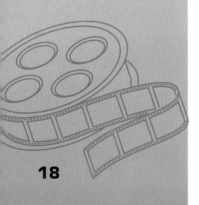

A

B

Goodbye!	Oh, no!	Fantastic! Here we are!	Please stop. We want to talk to you.	What's that?
We are going to Mars. I can't believe it!	Don't shoot! We come in peace.	It's completely empty!	Blobbity blobbity blob!	Stop. Who are you?

C

The space crew wave goodbye.	They meet a group of aliens who have got weapons.	After 24 days they land on Mars.	The alien runs away and they chase it.	They leave the spacecraft and see an alien.

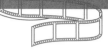

Can you picture it?

Language focus
reading descriptive language

Key vocabulary
vocabulary for describing people and places, e.g. *cruel, eyebrows, snake-like, surrounded, untidy, waves*

Skills focus
reading

Multiple intelligences
visual, linguistic and intrapersonal

Level
intermediate

Time
45 minutes

Preparation
one photocopy for each student. Students will also need a plain sheet of paper each to draw on.

Extra notes
It would be nice to have coloured pencils/pens available for this activity.

Warm-up

❶ Ask students to describe their favourite characters in films they have seen. You could begin by describing your favourite character as a model. Collect useful vocabulary on the board, revising language for describing people and clothes. Elicit language not just for the heroes, but for villains too.

❷ Go on to elicit language to describe the sets in films – the places where the action takes place like haunted houses, alien planets, etc.

Main activity

❶ Give each student an activity sheet and explain that the texts are extracts from books that are going to be made into films. Tell students they must imagine they work in the film business and help design sets and decide how characters are dressed and made-up. Explain that they have to make drawings that will be used to either design a set or to prepare the costume or make-up that a character will use.

❷ Tell students to read the six descriptions and choose the one they find most vivid and they wish to draw. While they are reading, they can refer to dictionaries or ask questions if there is vocabulary they don't understand.

❸ Tell students to draw their picture on a separate piece of paper. Hand paper out to students if they do not have their own.

❹ If any students particularly do not want to draw, they can pair up with another student and help or advise them.

Follow-up

◯ Pin the completed pictures around the classroom and ask students to compare how the written word has been depicted. They could vote for their favourites.

◯ Alternatively, with a group that is confident at speaking, you can pretend to be the film director and ask them to present their sketch to you and explain their vision of the character or scene.

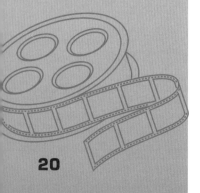

Film 2.1 Can you picture it?

Madame La Knife

She was tall and slim, but you could see she was very strong. Her blonde hair was very short. Her thin eyebrows sat over small, snake-like eyes. Her nose was straight and her lips thin, and her smile was always cold and cruel. She wore high heels, a straight skirt and a black jacket that had ten large metal buttons. Her right hand held the famous knife. It was long, sharp and dripping with blood.

....

Captain Johnny Ocean

He had a red scarf tied across his head, but his long hair fell on his shoulders in an untidy mess. Around his eyes were dark circles, and his moustache and beard were dark and untidy too. Under his right eye was the long scar from a fight he had had as a young man. His leather boots reached his knees, his trousers were dark and dirty and his shirt loose and baggy with dark stains on it. In his left hand he held his sword, and looked ready to fight.

....

The Amazing Bulk

It was always a shock to see him. His skin was bright orange and he was huge – the largest person you could imagine. His head was almost square and his forehead was large. His small eyes almost disappeared under thick, bushy eyebrows. His nose was round, his teeth were broken and crooked and he never smiled.
His body was like a rock, hard and muscular, his arms sticking out at his sides. His ragged clothes looked silly, as they were far too small for his enormous body.

....

The House of Horror

It sat on the top of a hill, far from any other building, dark clouds behind it. A few dead trees stood to the right with big black birds circling over them. The large house looked grey and old. You could only see four windows on the second floor. The glass in the windows was broken and there was no light within them. A fence surrounded the building but the gate stood open. A path led to the huge wooden door, which was closed.

....

Paradise Beach

The beach was long and wide. The sea was calm and the waves crashed gently on the shore, where you could see sea shells and crabs. There were many palm trees on the beach and the coconuts they had dropped were lying about. An expensive-looking yacht was sailing towards the beach and a few small fishing boats lay by the water's edge, their nets drying in the sun. The sun shone brightly and there were only a few small clouds in the sky.

....

Planet Borg

As our spacecraft was landing we could see the planet well. There were many hills covered in what looked like yellow grass and small red bushes. In the middle of the hills there was a flat area where the city lay. The buildings were all different, some short and round, some tall and straight, some even pyramid shaped or even shaped like stars. Every building had many windows and there was smoke or steam coming out of some of them. You couldn't see any people, but there were flying machines in the sky which looked like snakes and were silver, but had no windows.

Little monsters

Language focus
descriptive vocabulary

Key vocabulary
black fingernails,
bloodshot eyes, bolts,
cloak, dangerous, evil
eyes, fangs, flat head,
friendly, fur, horns,
pointed ears, powerful,
scales, scar, scary, sharp
teeth, webbed feet

Skills focus
writing and listening

Multiple intelligences
visual, linguistic and
interpersonal

Level
intermediate

Time
45 minutes

Preparation
one photocopy, cut into
Parts A and B, for each
student. Students will
also need a plain sheet of
paper each to draw on.

Warm-up

❶ Ask students if they have seen any films with monsters in. Elicit the names of the monsters, and some descriptions.

❷ Give students Part A of the activity sheet. Ask if any of the students recognise any of the pictures, and elicit what they know about these monsters.

Main activity

❶ Give students Part B of the activity sheet. Ask students to look at the vocabulary and match the words to the appropriate monsters. Explain that they may not be able to use all the words.

❷ Check their answers, and accept all reasonable answers.

❸ Elicit some sentences describing the monsters on the sheet, using the vocabulary in Part B. Write up the following sentence stems on the board:
It's got …
It's …
It looks like …
It seems …
It's the most …
It's wearing …

❹ Ask students to work in pairs and think of any other vocabulary that could go with these sentence stems to describe different monsters. Collate this vocabulary on the board and check that students understand and can say the new words. Encourage students to be creative with language and if they aren't sure of the English words allow them to look up words in dictionaries.

❺ Explain to students that they are going to think of a monster and draw it, then describe it in words.

❻ Ask students to work alone and draw their own monster. Tell them they must not show their picture to anyone else. Set a time limit of five minutes for this.

❼ Once students have finished their pictures, put them into pairs and tell them not to show each other their pictures. They should take turns to describe their monster to their partner, and their partner must produce a drawing based on the description.

❽ Students can compare their picture of their partner's monster with the original picture.

Follow-up

○ Students could redraw and label their own monster at home. These monster posters could become a nice classroom display.

○ Alternatively, students could write a paragraph describing a monster.

○ Students could also write scenes from films where their monsters appear, and act them out for fun in class.

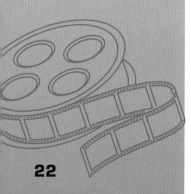

A

B

horns	scar	flat head
scales	friendly	**fur**
black fingernails	evil eyes	**webbed feet**
scary	FANGS	powerful
bloodshot eyes	**bolts**	*dangerous*
pointed ears	*cloak*	sharp teeth

Film crossword

Language focus
general film vocabulary

Key vocabulary
actor, camera, cartoon, cinema, comedy, cowboy, director, historical, horror, make-up, movie, science fiction, script, spy, star, war

Skills focus
vocabulary building

Multiple intelligences
linguistic and visual

Level
intermediate

Time
30 minutes

Preparation
one photocopy, cut into Parts A and B, for each pair of students. You could also make an OHT of the completed crossword.

Extra notes
This activity can be used with higher levels too, to revise film vocabulary.

Warm-up

❶ Put the students into pairs and give each pair Part A of the activity sheet. Ask students to look at the pictures and try to think of the English words for them.

❷ Elicit some possible answers from the class but don't write the words on the board, and don't tell students if they are correct or not. Students will be able to check their answers in the crossword activity.

❸ If students are struggling to think of the words, you could allow them to use their dictionaries to find any they do not know.

Main activity

❶ Give each pair Part B of the activity sheet. Point out the clues, and make sure that students understand the words *across* and *down*.

❷ Point out the anagrams, and tell students that they can use these, as well as the clues and the pictures, to find the answers.

❸ Ask the students to work in their pairs and complete the crossword.

❹ To check the answers quickly, put up an OHT of the completed crossword on the board and allow students to check their own answers. Drill the pronunciation of any words that are new to students.

Answers
Across: 2 camera, 3 make-up, 6 science fiction, 10 war, 13 cartoon, 14 spy

Down: 1 star, 2 cinema, 3 movie, 4 actor, 5 horror, 7 cowboy, 8 comedy, 9 director, 11 script, 12 historical

Follow-up

○ Invite one student at a time to come up to the front of the class.

○ Point to one of the pictures at the top of the activity sheet, without letting any of the other students see which picture you are pointing at, and ask the student to mime the word.

○ The other students must try to guess which word is being mimed.

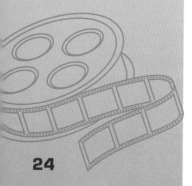

Film crossword

A

| 2 Across | 3 Across | 13 Across | 14 Across |

| 2 Down | 5 Down | 9 Down | 11 Down |

✂ -

B

Across

2 a machine that takes pictures and makes films (**aemarc**)
3 actors wear this on their faces in a film (**pameuk**)
6 a film with aliens and spaceships (**neecsic tinfcio**)
10 a film with soldiers and fighting (**raw**)
13 a film with moving pictures, not real people (**rotocan**)
14 James Bond is a ___. (**pys**)

Down

1 the most important actor in the film (**rats**)
2 a place where you watch films (**manice**)
3 the American word for film (**veomi**)
4 a person who acts in films (**corat**)
5 a film with monsters like Dracula to scare you (**roorhr**)
7 a film with horses, guns and American Indians (**woobcy**)
8 a film that makes you laugh (**demyco**)
9 the person who tells actors what to do in a film (**todrirec**)
11 the words that the actors read and say in a film (**tipscr**)
12 a film about the past (**calhisitor**)

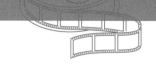

Which film?

Language focus
writing film blurbs

Key vocabulary
animated, blurb, classic, exotic location, road trip, romantic comedy, silent movie

Skills focus
reading and writing

Multiple intelligences
visual, linguistic and interpersonal

Level
intermediate

Time
45 minutes

Preparation
one photocopy of activity sheet A and B for each pair of students

Warm-up

❶ Ask students what films they have seen at the cinema recently.

❷ Ask them if they noticed the posters for these films. Elicit some descriptions of posters, and elicit the word *blurb*. Make sure that students understand what this is (a brief description advertising the film).

Main activity

❶ Put students into pairs and give each pair activity sheet A. Write these questions on the board:
What type of film is each film poster for?
What do you think happens in each film?
Which film would you like to see?
Ask students to look at the film posters and discuss the questions in their pairs.

❷ Hand out activity sheet B. Explain that this contains the titles of the films, and blurbs for the films.

❸ Ask students to write the correct title on each film poster. Tell them there are more titles than posters. Do not check answers at this stage.

❹ Ask students to match the blurbs to the film posters. Tell them there are more blurbs than posters. Do not check answers at this stage.

❺ Put pairs of students together to form groups of four. Ask them to compare their ideas and explain their choices. Then check answers with the class.

Answers					
1	l	Edward Scissorhands	5	k	Cleopatra
2	a	The Kid	6	i	Pirates of the Caribbean
3	c	The Day the Earth Stood Still	7	f	Goldeneye
4	d	The Simpsons	8	e	King Kong

❻ In their pairs, students choose a film they know and write a blurb for it. Tell them not to let other students hear what they are doing.

❼ When they have finished, ask each pair to read out their blurb. See if the class can guess which film it is describing. The class could vote for the best blurb.

Follow-up

○ Refer students back to the film posters, and ask them which they think is the oldest, and which the most modern. Tell them that the oldest was made in 1921, and the most modern in 2007.

○ Ask them to work in their pairs again and put the posters in order, from the oldest to the most modern.

○ Check answers. Ask students how they think film posters have changed over time.

Answers			
1921	The Kid	1990	Edward Scissorhands
1933	King Kong	1995	Goldeneye
1951	The Day the Earth Stood Still	2003	Pirates of the Caribbean 1
1963	Cleopatra	2007	The Simpsons

○ Alternatively, students could design their own posters for either a real or imaginary film, with visuals and blurb.

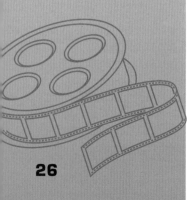

A

B

Titles

The Day the Earth Stood Still   Men from Mars   **The Kid**

Cleopatra   **Edward Scissorhands**   **The Simpsons**

Father and Son   **Pirates of the Caribbean**

King Kong   **Goldeneye**   Egypt   **M is for Murder**

Blurbs

a
This classic comedy starring the king of silent movies will make you laugh and cry …

b
Take a boy, a girl and a baby elephant, and you're sure to have some fun adventures. You will love this surprising romantic comedy.

c
No one knew they existed, until they came – the creatures from outer space who came to attack Earth.

d
You know he's bad, but you still love him. Our favourite animated hero hits the big screen.

e
He looks fierce, but this monster has a heart of gold and will do anything for the woman he loves.

f
Gorgeous women, exotic locations, dramatic car chases and explosions – he's back!

g
An old car, four friends and a lot of laughs. This comedy about a crazy road trip taken by four students will have you laughing out loud.

h
A visitor to a small town is not who she seems. Look out when people start disappearing …

i
Adventure on the sea – with sword fights, a love story and a loveable villain. Prepare to find treasure!

j
He seems like an ordinary guy, but he has extraordinary powers. Does he have the power to save the world from destruction?

k
When a queen falls in love in Ancient Egypt …

l
The story of an uncommonly gentle man, who happens to have scissors for hands …

Say it with feeling!

Language focus
language used in films

Key vocabulary
alive, escape, favourite, funniest, poison, prefer, save

Skills focus
speaking and intonation

Multiple intelligences
linguistic, kinaesthetic, musical and interpersonal

Level
intermediate

Time
45 minutes

Preparation
one photocopy of the board for each group of 4 or 5 students; one photocopy of activity sheet B cut up into cards, for each group. If possible, photocopy the cards onto card rather than paper. Each group will also need a photocopy of the rules.

Warm-up

❶ Write these sentences on the board:
Quick! The ship is on fire! / We've saved the world! / I'll never see him again! / You are wonderful!

Ask the students how the people saying these sentences feel, and how they would say them. Elicit that people would be feeling emotions such as fear, happiness, sadness or love, and this would be reflected in the intonation.

❷ Model the pronunciation and intonation of the sentences, exaggerating the intonation so that students can copy you. Drill the sentences with the class.

❸ Write on the board: *He's got a car!* Say the sentence with different types of intonation, for example as if you are happy, excited or in love, and get students to copy you.

❹ Explain to students that they are going to play a game in which they have to say sentences with particular types of intonation.

Main activity

❶ Pre-teach the key vocabulary and go through the language that students need to play the game: *flip the coin, move forward/back, pick a question, perform, as if you are in love, in pain, a monster, a hero*

❷ Put students into groups of four or five and hand out the board game. Hand out each set of cards in turn so that students can place them on the correct place on their board.

❸ Explain the rules of the game, or hand out a copy of the rules to each group. Students then play the game in their groups.

Follow-up

◉ Put students into small groups and ask them to write a short scene from a film using some of the lines from the game and adding their own ideas. Groups could read out their scenes to the class, speaking with the appropriate intonation.

Rules for Say it with feeling!

1 Each player must use a marker (e.g. a coin, button, pen top) and place it on the *Start here* space.

2 Take it in turns to flip a coin. If it is 'heads', move forward one square. If it is 'tails', move forward two squares.

3 When you land on a **?** square, pick a question from the pile of **?** cards and answer it.

4 When you land on a *Perform* square, pick a *Perform* card from the pile and a *Line* card. Say the line on the *Line* card in the way that is shown on the *Perform* card.

5 If you cannot answer a question, or do not perform well enough, you miss a turn.

6 The winner is the first student to go right round the board.

From *Film, TV and Music* © Cambridge University Press 2009 **PHOTOCOPIABLE**

A

?	Perform	?	Go back three squares
Perform	Line cards	? cards	?
Move forward two squares			Perform
?	Perform cards		?
Perform	?	FINISH	START HERE ↑

B

PERFORM CARDS	LINE CARDS	? CARDS
Sadly	"Who are you?"	**?** Who are the best actors in your country?
Happily	"Where is the body?"	**?** Name three things you can see in a cowboy film
As if you are in pain	"The money is not in the bag."	**?** Name three cinema monsters
As if you are a detective	"I love you very much."	**?** Do you prefer going to the cinema or watching films at home? Why?
As if you are in love	"There's poison in the tea."	**?** Who would you give an Oscar to this year?
As if you are frightened	"We must escape as soon as possible."	**?** What is your favourite film? Why?
As if you are a monster	"I think it's still alive!"	**?** What's the funniest film you have ever seen?
As if you are a hero	"Don't worry. I'll save you!"	**?** Would you like to work in films? Why?

Title, character, action

Language focus
talking about films

Key vocabulary
action, character, line, location

Skills focus
speaking and writing

Multiple intelligences
linguistic and interpersonal

Level
intermediate

Time
30 minutes

Preparation
one photocopy, cut up into cards, for each group of 4 students; one photocopy of the rules for each group

Extra notes
In this game, students have to judge whether their classmates have given an acceptable answer. This allows them to take responsibility, make judgements and exercise their sense of fairness. Of course, the teacher makes the final decision in any disagreement.

Warm-up

❶ Elicit some types of film, for example: *horror film, action film, comedy,* and write them on the right side of the board.

❷ On the left side of the board, write the following words:
Title, Action, Line, Object, Character, Location

❸ Choose one of the types of film, e.g. *horror film.* Point to the words on the left of the board and elicit things that are typical for this type of film, by saying for example:
Give me an example of a typical title of a horror film.
Give me an example of something that typically happens (Action).
Give me an example of a line someone might say. etc.

Make sure students understand all the key words on the board.

Main activity

❶ Put students into groups of four, and explain that they are going to play a game.

❷ Give each group a set of A cards and a set of B cards.

❸ Explain the rules, or hand out a copy of the rules to each group and give students time to read them.

❹ Students play the game in their groups.

Follow-up

○ For homework, students could write a short description of a film they have seen using the language they have been using in the game.

Rules for Title, character, action

1 Put the cards in two piles, face down on the table. Take it in turns to pick up a card from pile A and one from pile B.

2 Respond to the prompts and give a suitable answer, e.g. A *War film*; B *Location* – give an example of a typical location in a war film, for example a jungle.

3 As a group, decide if the answer is acceptable, and if it is give one point.

4 You cannot give an answer that has already been given.

5 The winner is the student with the most points at the end.

From *Film, TV and Music* © Cambridge University Press 2009 **PHOTOCOPIABLE**

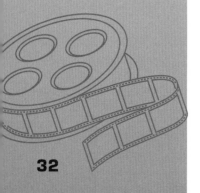

A

Cowboy film	War film	Horror film
Comedy	Cartoon	Spy film
Science fiction film	Love film	Action film

B

Title	**Object**
Action	**Character**
Line	**Location**

Scary or weird?

Language focus
reading about film genres

Key vocabulary
language for describing films and film genres

Skills focus
reading and speaking

Multiple intelligences
linguistic, visual and interpersonal

Level
upper intermediate

Time
60 minutes

Preparation
one photocopy, cut into Parts A and B, for each pair of students. If possible, bring in spooky atmospheric music to play during the warm-up.

Extra notes
Dictionaries should be available for each group in case they want to check any vocabulary during the reading phase.

Warm-up

❶ Ask the students to decide if they prefer horror or science fiction films and thus divide them into two groups. You may have to make some adjustments to make sure that the two groups are equal in number. Put students who have chosen the same genre into pairs. Ask each pair to create a mind map of words, ideas and pictures associated with the genre they have chosen. If you have any music that is spooky or perhaps the soundtrack of a horror or science-fiction film to play in the background, that would be great at setting the atmosphere. Allow five to ten minutes for this.

❷ Ask students to leave their mind maps on their table and to walk around the classroom looking at other students' mind maps. If they see anything they do not understand, they can make a note and when they have looked at all the mind maps and have returned to their seats, they can ask groups to explain what they have not understood. They can then add these words to their own mind maps if appropriate.

Main activity

❶ Give each student the appropriate activity sheet.

❷ Tell students to stay in the same pairs, so they are working with someone who has the same activity sheet as them. Tell them to work together to read their texts and prepare answers to the questions. Encourage them to write answers in their own words rather than just copying from the texts. Explain that some answers are in the text, but some rely on their own ideas.

❸ When students have prepared their answers, tell them to look at their text again and pick out any vocabulary or expressions from their text that they could add to their mind maps.

❹ Ask a pair of students who read about horror films to team up with a pair who read about science fiction films. Tell them to ask and answer the questions on the activity sheets.

❺ Ask groups to report back to the class on their discussions.

Follow-up

○ In the final paragraph of each text, the first film ever made in this genre is briefly described. Ask students to work in their groups of four and choose one of the films. Tell them to imagine what this film would have looked like and plan a scene from the film, using vocabulary and expressions from their mind maps.

○ Students can act out their scenes for each other

○ Alternatively, using the pictures on the page for ideas, students can design a film poster for these original films.

A

Horror films

Horror films are designed to frighten us and entertain us at the same time. The stories are typically based around strange or unreal events, and often have the feel of a terrible nightmare. The main characters are usually horrible creatures like vampires, madmen, devils and monsters, and the films may contain scenes of violence or death.

So why do people enjoy watching horror films? Psychologists believe that people enjoy being scared when they know that there is no real danger. Real fear is not enjoyable, but horror films allow us to experience the thrill of being frightened from the safety of our cinema seat. The other important thing that allows us to enjoy horror films is knowing that the ending will be happy. In horror films, the monster or madman is always defeated in the end.

The heroes in horror films are usually ordinary people, who become caught up in a nightmare situation. They try to escape but cannot, and in the end they have to find the courage within themselves to stand up to the horror and defeat it.

The earliest horror films were set in spooky old mansions or castles, where horrible monsters lay hiding. They used fake blood and a bit of scary music to create the atmosphere of fear. Nowadays, more modern horror films may use different locations, different types of monsters, and much more sophisticated special effects. But the basic story has not changed – ordinary people overcoming their fears to defeat something terrifying and horrific.

Horror films started over a hundred years ago. The first horror movie, only about three minutes long, was made in 1896 and was called *The Devil's Castle*. It told the story of a remote castle inhabited by evil vampires.

Questions

1   What kinds of characters do you typically find in horror films?
2   Why do people enjoy watching horror films?
3   How have horror films changed over time?
4   What was the first horror film?
5   Do you enjoy horror films? Why/Why not?
6   What other genres of film do you enjoy? What is your favourite genre? Why?

B

Science fiction films

Science fiction films are usually a mixture of science and imagination. They are often set in a future time or on a distant planet, and may involve time travel or journeys through outer space. Typical characters might include strange creatures from outer space or mutant monsters created by mad scientists in their laboratories of the future.

So why do people enjoy watching science fiction films? The answer may be that science fiction blends fiction and adventure with real possibility, and shows us things that could actually happen in the future if technology continues to develop. They open up the possibility of space travel and other worlds in the universe. They also warn us of the dangers of taking science too far – they show that technology has the power to destroy the Earth and human life.

The early science fiction films told the story of journeys to the Moon or Mars. They relied on simple filming techniques and a few crude special effects. More modern science fiction films, like the *Star Wars* movies, have been remarkable for their wonderful special effects, making weird creatures that look and sound as if they are real. More modern films also use more modern science in their plots, like the effects of a nuclear war or the possibilities of genetic engineering.

The very first science fiction film was made in 1902. It lasted for 14 minutes and was called *Voyage to the Moon*. It told the story of people's first journey to the moon, using the techniques of the time to produce scenes of people walking on the moon.

Questions

1   What kinds of characters do you typically find in science fiction films?
2   Why do people enjoy watching science fiction films?
3   How have science fiction films changed over time?
4   What was the first science fiction film?
5   Do you enjoy science fiction films? Why/Why not?
6   What other genres of film do you enjoy? What is your favourite genre? Why?

Do you agree?

Language focus
agreeing and disagreeing

Key vocabulary
censorship, computer-generated special effects, copy, role, role model, swearing, violence

Skills focus
speaking

Multiple intelligences
linguistic and interpersonal

Level
upper intermediate

Time
45 minutes

Preparation
one photocopy of each set of cards, cut up, for each group of 4 students; one photocopy of the rules for each group

Extra notes
Using the opinion cards helps students see an argument from different perspectives. This is a particularly useful skill when writing compositions that require a balanced argument. If some students feel this is too difficult, allow them to choose whether to offer their own opinion or that on the card.

Warm-up

❶ Write the following statement on the board: *Watching films is a waste of time.* Ask students to give their opinions.

❷ Elicit language for agreeing and disagreeing, and elicit ways in which you can agree or disagree strongly or not so strongly. For example:
I agree/disagree.
You may have a point.
You're probably right.
That's not really the case.
That's not always true.
I'm not sure.
Absolutely!
I totally agree with you!
I really can't agree with you there.
Surely you don't think ... !

❸ Model the pronunciation of the expressions, and the intonation used to agree or disagree strongly.

❹ Pre-teach the key vocabulary if necessary.

Main activity

❶ Explain to students that they are going to play a game in which they must give their opinions and agree and disagree with each other.

❷ Put students into groups of four, and give each group a set of the cards.

❸ Explain the rules, or hand out a copy of the rules to each group.

❹ Make sure students understand that they should express the opinion shown on the card even if they do not agree with it. Tell them they must participate in all the discussions. Encourage students to use the expressions on the board.

❺ Students play the game in their groups.

Follow-up

○ Tell students to choose one of the statements and write a short paragraph arguing either in favour of it or against it.

○ Students can read each other's paragraphs and vote for the best argument.

Rules for Do you agree?

1 Put the two piles of cards face down in front of you on the table.

2 Pick up one *Discussion* card and turn it over, so that everyone in the group can see it.

3 Shuffle the *Opinion* cards and hand one to each player.

4 Conduct a discussion about the subject on the *Discussion* card. Each student must express the opinion on their *Opinion* card.

5 When the discussion is finished, turn over the next *Discussion* card.

6 Collect up the *Opinion* cards, shuffle them, and hand them out again.

7 Continue discussing the different topics until you have discussed them all.

From *Film, TV and Music* © Cambridge University Press 2009 **PHOTOCOPIABLE**

Discussion cards:

Film stars get paid too much.	There is too much violence in modern films.
Films should not be more than 60 minutes long.	Young people today are influenced too much by films.
Tickets to the cinema are too expensive.	Parents should decide what films their children see or don't see until children reach the age of 18.
There should be no smoking or swearing in films as children copy that behaviour.	Seeing thin and beautiful female film stars makes girls unhappy with the way they look.
Film stars should try to be better role models for young people.	There should be no censorship in the cinema.
Children under 16 should not be allowed to see horror films.	All films should be made in black and white.
There aren't enough interesting roles for women in films.	Local films are much better than Hollywood films.
It's better to watch DVDs or videos at home than go out to the cinema.	Computer-generated special effects are ruining cinema as all the images can be improved by the computer.

Opinion cards:

AGREE	DISAGREE
DISAGREE STRONGLY	AGREE STRONGLY
ASK THE OTHER PEOPLE IN YOUR GROUP LOTS OF QUESTIONS	YOU DON'T HAVE A STRONG OPINION ON THIS SUBJECT

Crazy film plots

Language focus
relative clauses

Skills focus
writing and speaking

Multiple intelligences
linguistic and visual

Level
upper intermediate

Time
30 minutes

Preparation
one photocopy, cut into
Parts A and B, for each
student

Warm-up

❶ Elicit from students any ridiculous or very funny film plots they have seen. These will be plots that are unbelievable or bizarre. These will most likely be comedies, but not necessarily.

❷ Write these ideas for a film plot on the board, or dictate them to the class:
George is a young boy.
He lives in Florida.
He's only four years old.
He was walking on the beach.
He found some buried treasure.

❸ Ask students to rewrite all the sentences as one sentence, using relative clauses. You could make it a race, to see who can produce the first grammatically correct answer.

> **Suggested answer**
> George, who is a young boy and lives in Florida, was walking on the beach when he found some buried treasure.

Main activity

❶ Give each student Part A of the activity sheet.

❷ Ask them to fill in the sheet. Tell them that if they cannot think of all the items beginning with the same letter, they can use a dictionary, ask you or ask the class.

❸ When students have finished, hand out Part B of the activity sheet and go through the example with the class. Tell students that they should now use the words they have written to make a similar sentence. Stress that they must make only one sentence and point out that by using relative clauses they can include all the words more easily. Put students into pairs so that they can help each other produce their sentences.

❹ Ask students to read their sentences to the class. Get the class to help you correct any mistakes in the relative clauses.

❺ Tell students to stay in their pairs. Explain that their two sentences are a major part of the plot of a new film. Together they have to discuss what the film is all about and how their sentences fit into the whole story.

❻ When they have decided on their film plots, get each pair to join up with another pair. They should tell each other the plots of their films. Explain that the pairs listening can ask questions.

Follow-up

○ Ask students to work in their pairs and design posters for their crazy films.

○ Alternatively, students could work in pairs and write a summary of their film plot. The summaries could be displayed on the classroom walls for all the class to read.

○ Students could also work in groups of up to six to create and act out a scene from their film in front of the rest of the class.

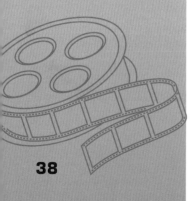

A

Fill in the gaps below. Don't share your ideas with anyone else!

Choose one letter of the alphabet: ☐

Write one word for each of the prompts below.

Each word must begin with the letter you have chosen.

A verb	....
An adjective	....
An adverb	....
A country	....
A person's name	....
A sport	....
A part of the body	....
An animal	....
A fruit or vegetable	....

✂ -

B

1 Look at this choice of words:

S – to speak – short – **suspiciously** – Sudan – Susan – skiing – shoulder – **squirrel** – strawberry

These were made into a sentence:

Susan, the short skiing champion from Sudan, suspiciously spoke to squirrels who sat on her shoulder while eating strawberries.

2 Create your sentence here. Use all your words and you may add others in order to make a sentence. Make only one sentence.

....

....

....

Stars in their eyes

Language focus
reading a biography

Key vocabulary
*agent, fearless,
idiosyncratic, lead
character, nominate,
recognition, star
in, sword, thrilled,
versatility, widespread*

Skills focus
reading and speaking

Multiple intelligences
linguistic, interpersonal
and mathematical

Level
upper intermediate

Time
45 minutes

Preparation
Each student will need
one photocopy of Part C,
and one photocopy
of Part A or Part B.

Extra notes
Have dictionaries
available for students to
use.

Warm-up

❶ Write the words *film stars* on the board. Invite your students to tell you who they consider to be film stars and why.

Main activity

❶ Write up the names *Keira Knightley* and *Johnny Depp* on the board and invite students to tell you anything they know about these actors.

❷ Divide the class into two groups, A and B, and explain that each group is going to read about a different actor. Give one group Part A of the activity sheet, and give the other group Part B.

❸ Put students into AA and BB pairs. Explain that the sentence beginnings in the left-hand column are in the correct order to form a text about each film star. Tell students to work in their pairs and find the correct ending for each sentence, then write out the full text in their notebooks.

❹ Check answers, then give a copy of Part C to every student. Ask students to continue working in pairs and fill in the grid with the key information they have just read. They should then work out how to ask questions to get the missing information to fill in the second part of their grid.

❺ Arrange students into new pairs so that a student A is with a student B. Tell students to ask and answer questions to exchange information and fill in the grid.

Answers

Keira Knightley

Keira Knightley was born in Teddington, England, on 22 March 1985. Keira showed an interest in acting when she was only three years old, but her parents didn't let her have an agent until she was six.
She first appeared in *Star Wars: Episode 1 – The Phantom Menace*, when she was just eleven. She was the maid to the lead character, Padmé, played by Natalie Portman. However, it wasn't until she starred in *Bend It Like Beckham* that she received widespread recognition. Her role in *Pirates of the Caribbean* confirmed her as a huge international star. The fearless Keira did all her own stunts in *Pirates of the Caribbean: Dead Man's Chest* – she was thrilled that she got to fight with a real sword! She has won several awards and she has been nominated for an Oscar for her acting in *Pride and Prejudice*.

Johnny Depp

Johnny Depp was born John Christopher Depp III on 9 June, 1963.
When Johnny was a child he had pet lizards that he trained to do tricks. Johnny's acting debut was in the classic horror film *A Nightmare on Elm Street* (1984).
He is famous for his versatility, acting in comedies, science-fiction, horror, drama and even children's films.
His fans love his idiosyncratic performances, such as the character Jack Sparrow in the *Pirates of the Caribbean* films. He is regularly voted by fans as the most popular and best-looking actor alive! He was nominated three times for Oscars in 2004, 2005 and 2008.

Follow-up

○ For homework, ask students to write a biography of their favourite film star, describing their life and explaining why they are important.

○ Students could read each other's biographies and vote for the best.

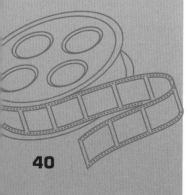

Film 3.4) Stars in their eyes

A

Keira Knightley

Keira Knightley was born in	confirmed her as a huge international star.
Keira showed an interest in acting when she was only three years old,	she was thrilled that she got to fight with a real sword!
She first appeared in *Star Wars: Episode 1 – The Phantom Menace*,	an Oscar for her acting in *Pride and Prejudice*.
However, it wasn't until she starred in *Bend It Like Beckham*	Teddington, England, on 22 March 1985.
Her role in *Pirates of the Caribbean*	that she received widespread recognition.
The fearless Keira did all her own stunts in *Pirates of the Caribbean: Dead Man's Chest* –	but her parents didn't let her have an agent until she was six.
She has won several awards and she has been nominated for	when she was just eleven. She was the maid to the lead character, Padmé, played by Natalie Portman.

✂ -

B

Johnny Depp

Johnny Depp was born John Christopher Depp III	as the most popular and best-looking actor alive!
When Johnny was a child, he had pet lizards	acting in comedies, science fiction, horror, drama and even children's films.
Johnny's acting debut was in the	three times for Oscars in 2004, 2005 and 2008.
He is famous for his versatility,	that he trained to do tricks.
His fans love his idiosyncratic performances,	such as the character Jack Sparrow in the *Pirates of the Caribbean* films.
He is regularly voted by fans	classic horror film *A Nightmare on Elm Street* (1984).
He was nominated	on 9 June, 1963.

✂ -

C

	Keira Knightley	Johnny Depp
Born?		
Acting career began when/how?		
Characters he/she plays/played?		
Achievements? Awards?		
Weird and wonderful facts?		

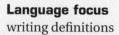

Film 3.5

I haven't a clue

Language focus
writing definitions

Key vocabulary
cameraman, cinema, cowboy, director, Frankenstein, genre, Hollywood, movie, Oscar, screenplay, secret agent, star, stuntman, subtitles, Superman

Skills focus
writing and speaking

Multiple intelligences
linguistic and interpersonal

Level
upper intermediate

Time
30 minutes

Preparation
one photocopy, cut into Parts A and B, for each pair of students

Extra notes
Have dictionaries available for students to use.

Warm-up

❶ Tell students that you have forgotten an English word and ask them to help you find it. Say: *It's a kind of film ..., it is scary ..., it often has monsters ..., 'Dracula' is one of these ...* etc. until someone says *horror film*.

❷ Explain that you have just been defining the word, so that they could guess it, and this is what they are going to be doing this lesson.

Main activity

❶ Explain to students that they are going to do a crossword in pairs, and they must write definitions to help their partner complete their crossword.

❷ Divide the class into two groups, A and B, and give each student the appropriate half of the crossword.

❸ Put students into AA and BB pairs. Tell them to look at the words that are already in their crossword, and create definitions or clues for them. Tell them they can use dictionaries to help them.

❹ Once they have completed their clues, tell them to show the clues to you so that you can check them before they move on to the next stage.

❺ When students are ready, put them into new pairs, with one A and one B student in each pair. Explain that they are going to ask each other for clues for the missing words in their crossword, and try to complete them.

❻ Write on the board: *What's one down? What's eleven across?* Point out that this is how they should ask for clues from their partner.

❼ Students then work in pairs to exchange their clues and try to complete their crosswords.

❽ Students can check their answers by looking at the words in their partner's crossword.

Follow-up

⭕ For homework, ask students to prepare five gapped sentences to test their classmates on the new vocabulary.

⭕ Students can then test each other in the next lesson.

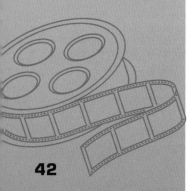

A

B

People and programmes

Language focus
vocabulary of TV
programmes and people

Key vocabulary
*actor, cookery
programme,
entertainment
programme, history
programme, music
programme, the news,
news reader, police
drama, presenter,
quiz show, sports
commentator, sports
programme, weather
report, wildlife
programme*

Skills focus
vocabulary building and
writing

Multiple intelligences
visual, linguistic and
interpersonal

Level
elementary

Time
30 minutes

Preparation
one photocopy for each
student

Extra notes
This activity can also be
used with higher levels
for revision.

Warm-up

❶ Ask students what their favourite TV programme is. Elicit some names of programmes, then ask what types of programmes they are, for example comedy programmes, entertainment programmes etc.

❷ Ask who is in the programmes. Elicit some names first, then ask what that person's role in the show is, for example the presenter.

Main activity

❶ Put students into pairs and give each student an activity sheet.

❷ Ask students to look at the programme words and match the pictures to the words. Tell them to write the number of each picture next to the correct word. Check answers and drill the pronunciation.

> **Answers**
> See answers below.

❸ Refer students to the people words, and get them to match these to the pictures. Explain that some words go with more than one picture. They should write the numbers of the correct pictures next to each word. Check answers and drill the pronunciation.

> **Answers**
> 1 wildlife programme, presenter   2 quiz show, quiz master
> 3 hospital drama, actor   4 history programme, presenter
> 5 the news, news reader   6 police drama, actor
> 7 music programme, presenter   8 sports programme, sports commentator
> 9 comedy show, comedian 10 cookery programme, TV chef
> 11 weather report, weather reporter
> 12 entertainment programme, presenter

❹ Write the following on the board:
I like ....s. / I'd like to be a(n) ....

Elicit which of the words on the sheet would fit into each sentence, e.g. *I like sports programmes* and *I'd like to be an actor.*

❺ Ask students to work individually and write four sentences using the sentence stems on the board. Tell them that two must be true, and two must be false.

❻ In pairs, students take turns to read out their sentences to their partner. Their partner must guess whether each sentence is true or not. Students can then walk around the class and talk to different classmates, repeating the activity.

Follow-up

○ Students could make posters about television, using some of their sentences. They can draw pictures to decorate their posters, or use pictures from magazines or the internet.

○ Alternatively, students could write a short paragraph saying what types of programmes they like and dislike.

Programmes

quiz show 2
wildlife programme
hospital drama
music programme
sports programme
entertainment programme
weather report
comedy show
police drama
history programme
the news
cookery programme

People

weather reporter
news reader
quiz master
presenter
actor
sports commentator
comedian
TV chef

Is it on every day?

Language focus
asking and answering
present tense questions

Key vocabulary
types of TV programmes;
days of the week; time
phrases; *exciting, funny,
interesting*

Skills focus
speaking

Multiple intelligences
linguistic and
interpersonal

Level
elementary

Time
30 minutes

Preparation
one photocopy for each
student; one photocopy
of the rules for each
group of 6 to 8 students

Extra notes
You could do activity
TV1.1 before you do
this one, to teach the
vocabulary of types
of programmes. This
activity also provides
a useful opportunity
to revise and practise
time phrases, e.g. *at six
o'clock, on Mondays,
in the evening* etc.

Warm-up

❶ Choose one student in the class. Tell them to think of their favourite TV programme, but not tell you what it is.

❷ Ask them yes/no questions to try to guess what it is, for example: *Is it on every day? Is it funny?* Encourage other students to join in and ask questions.

❸ Tell students they are going to play a guessing game about TV programmes.

Main activity

❶ Hand out the activity sheets and refer students to the questions. Explain that they are going to use these questions, but must first unjumble them. Put students into pairs to unjumble the questions and write the correct question underneath each jumbled one.

❷ Check answers, and tell students to make sure they have written each question correctly. You could prepare an OHT with the answers. Point out that some of the questions begin *Is it …* and some begin *Do you …* Elicit that the answer to all the questions can be *yes, no, maybe* or *sometimes.* Drill some of the questions with the class.

> **Answers**
> 1 Is it a music programme?   2 Do you see animals on the programme?
> 3 Is it on every day?   4 Is it for children?
> 5 Do you see famous people on the programme?   6 Is it interesting?
> 7 Do you watch it in the evening?   8 Is it funny?
> 9 Is it on TV on Sundays?   10 Is it exciting?   11 Is it on at six o'clock?
> 12 Do you see real people on the programme?

❸ Ask students to continue working in pairs and write three more questions. Remind them that they must be questions that you can answer with *yes, no, sometimes* etc. Ask some pairs to read their questions out, and write useful ones on the board.

❹ Arrange the class into groups of six or eight. Hand out copies of the rules, and go through them as a class. Students then play the game in their groups.

Follow-up

○ Ask students to write about their favourite programme, using the language they have used for the game, for example:

.... is on TV on Mondays in the evening. It's a sports programme. It's very interesting.

Rules for Is it on every day?

1 Players take turns to think of a programme.

2 Other players ask questions and try to guess.

3 When one player thinks they know the answer, they can say what they think the programme is.

4 If they are correct, they get a point. If they are wrong, they lose a point.

5 The winner is the player with the most points at the end of the game.

---

1   it / Is / programme / music / a

_____?

2   animals / you / Do / on / see / programme / the

_____?

3   every / day / on / Is / it

_____?

4   children / it / for / Is

_____?

5   famous / people / see / programme / Do / you / the / on

_____?

6   interesting / Is / it

_____?

7   evening / Do / watch / it / the / you / in

_____?

8   it / funny / Is

_____?

9   Sundays / on / TV / on / Is / it

_____?

10 it / Is / exciting

_____?

11 at / o'clock / six / on / it / Is

_____?

12 real / people / programme / on / the / Do / see / you

_____?

13 _____?

14 _____?

15 _____?

My favourite programme

_____

_____

_____

_____

_____

Give me a clue!

Language focus
vocabulary of TV
programmes and people

Key vocabulary
*actor, chef, comedian,
comedy, commentator,
cookery, drama, history,
news, news reader,
presenter, programme,
weather, wildlife*

Skills focus
writing clues

Multiple intelligences
linguistic, visual and
interpersonal

Level
elementary

Time
30 minutes

Preparation
one photocopy, cut into
Parts A and B, for each
pair of students

Extra notes
This activity revises the
vocabulary students
learned in activity 1.1,
so it is advisable to do
activity 1.1 first.

Warm-up

❶ Tell students they are going to revise television vocabulary through a crossword. Show them an example of a crossword, or draw a rough crossword on the board, and teach the words *clue, down* and *across*.

❷ Explain to students that they will be giving each other clues for the words in the crossword. Elicit different ways they can use to give clues, for example by speaking, drawing or miming.

Main activity

❶ Divide the class into A and B students.

❷ Give out the activity sheets and explain to students that they already have half the words in their crossword, and they must work in pairs to complete it. They must give their partner clues for the words they already have, and use their partner's clues to find their missing words.

❸ Put students into groups of three or four, with As working together and Bs working together. Make sure they have scrap paper to draw on and a pencil if needed. Tell them they should brainstorm ways of giving clues for their words. Monitor and help at this stage, giving students ideas for clues if they are struggling, and checking that their clues are accurate. Get them to write their clues on their sheets.

❹ Put students into pairs, with one A and one B in each pair. Tell them to sit facing each other, so they cannot see each other's crosswords. Explain that they are going to take it in turn to ask their partner for clues, and model the type of questions they will ask, for example *What's three across?*

❺ Students exchange their clues and complete their crosswords. They can check their answers by looking at their partner's crossword.

Follow-up

○ Ask students to think of other words they know relating to television and write each one on a piece of paper. Collect these papers and jumble them up or put them in a bag or hat. Ask students to come up to the front of the class one at a time and select one word from the bag. They then give a spoken clue or draw or mime a clue for the rest of the class to guess the word.

○ This could be done as a team game in two or more teams. Each team takes it in turns to play, with one of the team giving a clue and the rest of the team trying to guess. Set a time limit of 30 seconds for their team mates to guess the word. The team scores one point if they guess within 30 seconds. If not, one of the other teams may try and, if they are right, they score an extra point.

A

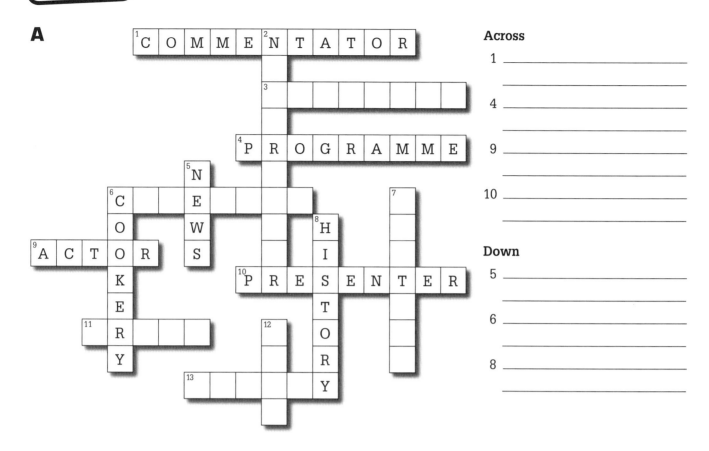

Across

1 _____

_____

4 _____

9 _____

_____

10 _____

_____

Down

5 _____

_____

6 _____

_____

8 _____

_____

✂ -

B

Across

3 _____

6 _____

_____

11 _____

13 _____

_____

Down

2 _____

_____

7 _____

_____

12 _____

_____

The weakest link

Language focus
present simple questions; superlatives

Key vocabulary
baseball, basketball, capital, desert, football, mountain, river, sport, star, team

Skills focus
speaking and listening

Multiple intelligences
linguistic and interpersonal

Level
elementary

Time
30 minutes

Preparation
one photocopy of Part A for each student; one photocopy of Part B, cut up into cards, for each group of 5 or 6 students

Extra notes
This activity will work best if students cannot hear what is being said by other groups, so groups should be as far away from each other as possible, and encouraged to speak quietly. You could play background music to prevent them hearing each other's answers.

Warm-up

1 Ask the students if they like watching TV quiz shows. Find out which are their favourite ones.

2 Give each student Part A of the activity sheet. Allow them time to read it, and explain the meaning of the expression *weakest link* (the person who is not as good as all the others). Point out that the woman who asks the question is very rude to people if they don't know an answer and this is part of the fun of the programme. Ask the students if there is a local version of *The Weakest Link* in their country or something similar.

3 Pre-teach or check understanding of the key vocabulary, and drill the pronunciation.

Main activity

1 Put students into groups of five or six. Explain that they are going to re-enact a TV quiz show in the style of *The Weakest Link*.

2 Ask each group to choose its quiz master. Explain that the quiz master must ask other students questions in turn. Tell the quiz master they should be tough and use the line *You are the weakest link* when someone makes a mistake. That player is then out of the game. The winner is the player who answers the most questions correctly, and is still in the game at the end.

3 Give a set of question cards to each quiz master.

4 Students work in their groups and play the game.

Follow-up

○ Tell students they are going to prepare their own TV quiz show. Put them into small groups and ask them to write their own questions on any categories they want.

○ Monitor the groups while they are writing their questions to ensure they are correct.

○ Ask the groups to decide if they want to use their questions to play *The Weakest Link* again, or play a different game, using different rules. If they want to use their own game and rules, they must think of a title for their show and decide on the rules of the game and a system of scoring.

○ Tell them to think about prizes too, to add to the fun.

○ Groups can invite other students to take part in their quiz show. If possible, record the quiz shows on video so that students can watch them later.

A

The Weakest Link

In the UK one of the most popular TV quiz shows is called *The Weakest Link*. The presenter, Anne Robinson, always wears black and never smiles. She is rude to the contestants and if they make a mistake she always says, 'You are the weakest link, goodbye' and they have to leave. Do you have a similar programme in your country?

B

What is the capital of the USA? Answer: Washington	**What is the biggest desert in the world?** Answer: The Sahara
What is the capital of China? Answer: Beijing	**What is the highest mountain in the world?** Answer: Mount Everest
What is the capital of Hungary? Answer: Budapest	**What is the longest river in the world?** Answer: The Nile
What is the capital of Egypt? Answer: Cairo	**What is the capital of Argentina?** Answer: Buenos Aires
What sport does Roger Federer play? Answer: Tennis	**What sport does Tiger Woods play?** Answer: Golf
What sport does Cristiano Ronaldo play? Answer: Football	**What sport does Barry Bonds play?** Answer: Baseball
How many people are there in a basketball team? Answer: five	**How many people are there in a football team?** Answer: 11
How many people are there in a baseball team? Answer: nine	**How many people are there in a tennis doubles match?** Answer: four (two against two)
Who is the star of the *Mission Impossible* films? Answer: Tom Cruise	**Who is the star of the *Indiana Jones* films?** Answer: Harrison Ford
Who is the star of the new *James Bond* films? Answer: Daniel Craig	**Who is the star of the *Matrix* films?** Answer: Keanu Reeves

Silent TV

Language focus
vocabulary of TV
programmes

Key vocabulary
*children's programme,
comedy, commercial,
cookery programme,
health programme,
hospital drama,
news, police drama,
sports programme,
weather report, wildlife
programme*

Skills focus
reading

Multiple intelligences
kinaesthetic, visual and
linguistic

Level
elementary

Time
30 minutes

Preparation
one photocopy, cut up
into cards, for the whole
class

Warm-up

❶ Tell the students that yesterday evening you had a problem with your television:
the picture was working, but there was no sound. Tell them that this is what you
saw on the TV. Mime some of the suggestions below or use your own ideas. Ask
students to guess what type of programme it is, and what is happening.
Someone playing tennis (a sports programme)
Someone reading the news (the news)
Someone committing a murder (a police drama)

❷ Elicit words for other types of programmes in order to revise all the necessary
vocabulary. Make sure you elicit or teach the programme types listed in the key
vocabulary.

Main activity

❶ Divide the class into two teams. Explain that students are going to mime
TV programmes. Other students from their team must guess the type of
programme and what is happening.

❷ If you have 14 or fewer students, give one miming card to each student. If you
have more than 14 students, put them into pairs and give each pair one miming
card. Tell them they must not show their instructions to anyone else.

❸ Allow students time to read and understand their instructions. Tell them they
can use dictionaries if they like, or they can ask you to explain words they don't
understand.

❹ Ask students to come out to the front of the class one at a time, or one pair at a
time, to perform their mimes. Their team has 60 seconds to guess the answer,
and after that time the other team can try to guess too. Teams score one point
every time they guess correctly.

Follow-up

○ Put students into groups of three or four, and ask each group to prepare three
mimes of their own to mime as a group.

○ Ask the class to vote for the best group mime.

You are a police officer. Someone is running away and you chase them. You catch them and arrest them. (police drama)	You are a champion racing driver. You win a race and then open a bottle of champagne. (sports programme)
You are playing golf. You hit the ball but miss the hole. (sports programme)	You are a TV chef making a cake. (cookery programme)
You are a doctor. You are doing an operation on someone to save their life. (hospital drama)	You are a police officer. You find a dead person in a room. You phone for help, then you look around carefully and find some clues on the floor. (police drama)
You are a football player. You are playing football, but the other team scores a goal. (sports programme)	You are on a TV commercial. You show how white and clean your clothes are when you use SuperClean! washing powder. (commercial)
You are a gym teacher. You show the people watching how to do exercises to stay healthy. (health programme)	You are a news reporter. There is a big fire in a building and you are giving a news report from the scene. (the news)
You are a comedian. You are walking down the street and you slip on a banana skin. (comedy)	You are a weather reporter. You are showing tomorrow's weather. It is very bad, with wind and rain. (weather report)
You are a clown. You are blowing up some balloons for children. You do funny things to make them laugh. (children's programme)	You are watching some monkeys in a tree and talking about them. One of them takes your hat. (wildlife programme)

TV 1.6

Talk, talk, talk!

Language focus
talking about habits and likes and dislikes

Key vocabulary
types of TV programmes, e.g.: *cookery programme, documentary, hospital drama, music programme, the news, police drama, reality TV show, quiz show, soap opera, wildlife programme*

Skills focus
speaking

Multiple intelligences
linguistic, kinaesthetic and interpersonal

Level
elementary

Time
45 minutes

Preparation
one photocopy of the board for each group of 4 students; one photocopy of the *Talk* cards, cut up, for each group; one photocopy of the rules for each group; each group will also need a coin to flip

Warm-up

❶ Ask a few individual students what kinds of TV programmes they enjoy watching and why.

❷ Explain that students are going to play a board game in English in which they have to talk about their television habits. Show the game to them. Tell them that in order to play the game they will need some English expressions.

❸ Write the following expressions on the board. Check or teach the meaning, then drill the expressions:
It's your/my turn.
It's heads/tails.
Well done.
Never mind.

❹ Revise the key vocabulary and teach any words students don't know.

Main activity

❶ Put students into groups of four and give each group a copy of the board and a set of cards.

❷ Give each group a copy of the rules and go through them with the class.

❸ Students play the game in their groups.

Follow-up

○ Ask students to use the language they have practised in the game to write a paragraph on their own TV habits.

○ Alternatively, students could work in groups and design a questionnaire to ask their classmates about their viewing habits. They could question each other, then present their findings to the class.

Rules for Talk, talk, talk!

1 Players start the game on the *Start* square.

2 Take it in turns to flip a coin. Move forward one square for 'heads', and two for 'tails'.

3 When you land on a square, follow the instructions or complete the sentence.

4 If you land on a *Talk* square, pick up a card. You must answer the question on the card, and must say at least three sentences.

5 If you do not say three sentences, you miss a turn.

6 You cannot give the same answer as another player.

7 The winner is the player who finishes first.

From *Film, TV and Music* © Cambridge University Press 2009 **PHOTOCOPIABLE**

START → FINISH	I usually watch ___	Talk	Miss a turn	Talk	I sometimes watch ___ on Saturdays	Talk	Have an extra turn
Talk	At the weekend I usually watch ___	Talk	Move forwards one space	I never watch ___	Talk	Move back three spaces
Miss a turn						
Move back two spaces						

TALK CARDS

Talk about soap operas.	Talk about documentaries you like.	Talk about sports programmes.	Talk about documentaries you don't like.
Talk about the news on TV.	Talk about programmes you watch at the weekend.	Talk about a programme you watch with your family.	Talk about wildlife programmes.
Talk about a programme your grandparents like.	Talk about hospital dramas.	Talk about a programme you think is boring.	Talk about reality TV shows.
Talk about a programme you think is interesting.	Talk about programmes your dad likes.	Talk about your favourite programme.	Talk about programmes you hate.
Talk about sports that you like watching on TV.	Talk about programmes you think are funny.	Talk about when you watch TV.	Talk about cookery programmes.
Talk about music programmes on TV.	Talk about quiz shows on TV.	Talk about police dramas.	Talk about films on TV.

What shall we watch?

Language focus
reading for key
information; negotiating

Key vocabulary
*cartoon, comedy, quiz
show, soap opera, wildlife
documentary*

Skills focus
reading and speaking

Multiple intelligences
linguistic, interpersonal
and kinaesthetic

Level
intermediate

Time
45 minutes

Preparation
one photocopy of
activity sheet A for each
student; one photocopy
of activity sheet B for
each group of 4 students

Warm-up

❶ Write on the board TV LISTINGS. Elicit the meaning, and ask students where they can find the TV listings (in newspapers and magazines, or on the internet).

❷ Ask students if they ever disagree with other people in their family about which programme to watch.

Main activity

❶ Give each student a copy of activity sheet A. Explain that this is a TV listing, but some information is missing. Ask students to work in pairs and add the missing information.

❷ Join up pairs of students so they are in groups of four. Get them to check their answers in their groups, then check with the class.

> **Answers**
> A 3   B 11   C 1   D 10   E 9   F 2   G 8   H 7   I 12   J 6   K 5   L 4

❸ Check that students understand everything on the sheet.

❹ Give a set of role-play cards to each group of four students, and ask them to share them out. Explain to students that they must pretend to be the person on their role-play card. Focus on the expressions used for persuasion. Explain that students can use these expressons during their discussions. Ask them to add some more expressions. Elicit some from the whole class and write useful ones on the board.

❺ Explain that each group is going to be spending their evening together tonight and these are the only TV channels they can watch. They all want to watch television but have different tastes in programmes. They have to try to convince the others in their group to watch the programmes they like. They must try to reach an agreement about what they are going to watch.

❻ Students do the role play in their groups.

❼ As an alternative to the role play, students can have the discussion as themselves, expressing their own opinions.

❽ Ask some groups to feed back to the class, and see how many managed to reach agreement.

Follow-up

◯ Ask students to imagine a perfect evening's television and to design the listings page for that evening.

◯ Encourage them to add illustrations and reviews – anything they feel is appropriate.

A

Channel 1	Channel 2	Channel 3
5.30 Local news and weather	5.45 The Juan & Mary Show – with special guest stars David Beckham & Justin Timberlake	5.20 Diet Doctors – H _____
6.00 Ready Cooks – A _____		6.15 International and local news
6.45 The Simpsons – cartoon comedy	6.45 Everybody Hates James – American comedy starring James Carter	7.15 Boxing – I _____
7.15 Westenders – B _____	7.15 Friends in the Big Apple – D _____	9.00 My Best Friend is an Alien – J _____
7.55 The African Elephant – C _____	7.45 Music TV – E _____	
9.00 Film – James Bond: The Spy who Ran Away	8.30 Football – F _____	10.00 What Do You Know? – K _____
11.00 Late night news and weather	10.30 Murder Express – G _____	10.45 The World Today – L _____

1   Some wonderful photography in this wildlife documentary about this magnificent animal.
2   This should be an exciting match, as Dynamo Kiev play Manchester United in the semi-final of the Champion's League.
3   Our two celebrity chefs are back and will show you some simple healthy meals to prepare.
4   An hour of discussions on Current Affairs, Politics and World News.
5   The most popular quiz show on TV is back. Six contestants test their general knowledge and try to win one of the many prizes. Tonight's special prize is a sports car.
6   Another episode of the comedy science fiction drama series. Tonight our hero Jake is taken to the alien planet for the first time.
7   The programme for people who want to lose weight and be healthy. Lots of advice on how to eat well and keep fit.
8   Another mysterious death for Detective Flynn to solve. This week, an old lady is found dead in a car park. Who is the killer?
9   Lots of information about the latest hits, and a live performance from The Kaiser Chiefs.
10   More American comedy about six friends sharing a flat in New York. Tonight Jenny breaks her leg, and Tom gets fed up with his job.
11   The popular soap opera about people living in the West End of London. Tonight Lady Claire declares her love for the postman. How will he react?
12   More exciting sport, with the world championship from Los Angeles.

B

A You love sport, and you hate soap operas. You think documentaries are boring, and you don't like wildlife programmes.

Some useful language of persuasion:

If we watch _____ at _____ o'clock, we could watch _____ after that.

I don't mind if we watch some _____, but could we please watch _____?

It would be so interesting to watch _____. I hear it's very good.

Add a few more expressions:

_____

_____

_____

B You love music programmes and murder mysteries. You don't really like wildlife programmes, and you find the news boring.

Some useful language of persuasion:

If we watch _____ at _____ o'clock, we could watch _____ after that.

I don't mind if we watch some _____, but could we please watch _____?

It would be so interesting to watch _____. I hear it's very good.

Add a few more expressions:

_____

_____

_____

C You love watching films, especially spy films. You also like soap operas. You don't like watching sport, and you don't mind news programmes.

Some useful language of persuasion:

If we watch _____ at _____ o'clock, we could watch _____ after that.

I don't mind if we watch some _____, but could we please watch _____?

It would be so interesting to watch _____. I hear it's very good.

Add a few more expressions:

_____

_____

_____

D You love wildlife programmes and programmes about health. You don't really like soap operas, but you don't mind films.

Some useful language of persuasion:

If we watch _____ at _____ o'clock, we could watch _____ after that.

I don't mind if we watch some _____, but could we please watch _____?

It would be so interesting to watch _____. I hear it's very good.

Add a few more expressions:

_____

_____

_____

Guess what I watch!

Language focus
asking and answering questions using different tenses

Key vocabulary
TV programme types; adverbs of frequency

Skills focus
speaking

Multiple intelligences
intrapersonal, interpersonal, linguistic and kinaesthetic

Level
intermediate

Time
45 minutes

Preparation
one photocopy for each student

Extra notes
It would be nice to have coloured pencils/pens available for the follow-up activity. Ask students in the previous lesson to bring them along, if none are available in school.

Warm-up

❶ Ask students to guess what you watched on TV last night. Then ask them to guess what kinds of programmes you like.

❷ Tell them if they are right or wrong, then explain that they are going to make similar guesses about other students in the class.

Main activity

❶ Give each student an activity sheet. Tell students they should choose three people in the class, and they are going to guess what types of programmes these people like. Encourage them not just to choose close friends, but also classmates who they do not know very well. Tell them to fill in the names of the three students they have chosen at the top of the page.

❷ Allow students time to read through the guesses they must make. Tell them they must guess whether each statement is True or False for each of the classmates they have chosen. Point out that the last one is blank. Tell them they must add one idea of their own.

❸ Tell students to make their guesses about the television habits of the three people they have chosen, and write True or False on the sheet. Make sure students understand that they are not allowed to ask the people, but must guess.

❹ Tell students that they are now going to ask questions to check whether they guessed correctly. Put students into pairs. Tell them to prepare each question and write it in the correct place on the sheet. Tell them to make sure they use the correct tense for each question and form the questions correctly.

❺ Check the questions with the class.

> **Answers**
> 1 Do you watch at least two hours of TV every day?
> 2 Were you watching the news last night at 9pm?
> 3 Do you have/Have you got your own TV in your bedroom?
> 4 Did you watch any sports programmes last weekend?
> 5 Have you ever watched a documentary on TV?
> 6 Would you like to work in TV?
> 7 Do you like watching TV while you are doing your homework?
> 8 Would you rather watch a crime drama than a documentary?

❻ Students now move around and question the people they made guesses about. They check against their guesses, and circle 'Right' or 'Wrong' for each question. The activity is finished when all students have spoken to all three of the classmates they have chosen.

❼ Just for fun, ask students to score themselves on the task, giving themselves one point for each correct guess they made. Check which students got the most points.

Follow-up

○ Ask students to choose one of the classmates they decided to guess about and to write a short paragraph about their TV habits. They could go back to them and ask more questions before writing.

○ Alternatively, ask students to create posters about their own TV habits, using the information and language they have been focusing on in class. They can write, draw pictures or use pictures from magazines or the internet.

	Classmate 1 _____	Classmate 2 _____	Classmate 3 _____
1 ... watches at least two hours of TV every day. _____ _____?	Guess: _____ Right/Wrong?	Guess: _____ Right/Wrong?	Guess: _____ Right/Wrong?
2 ... was watching the news last night at 9pm. _____ _____?	Guess: _____ Right/Wrong?	Guess: _____ Right/Wrong?	Guess: _____ Right/Wrong?
3 ... has their own TV in their bedroom. _____ _____?	Guess: _____ Right/Wrong?	Guess: _____ Right/Wrong?	Guess: _____ Right/Wrong?
4 ... watched sports programmes last weekend. _____ _____?	Guess: _____ Right/Wrong?	Guess: _____ Right/Wrong?	Guess: _____ Right/Wrong?
5 ... has never watched a documentary on TV. _____ _____?	Guess: _____ Right/Wrong?	Guess: _____ Right/Wrong?	Guess: _____ Right/Wrong?
6 ... would like to work in TV. _____ _____?	Guess: _____ Right/Wrong?	Guess: _____ Right/Wrong?	Guess: _____ Right/Wrong?
7 ... likes watching TV while doing their homework. _____ _____?	Guess: _____ Right/Wrong?	Guess: _____ Right/Wrong?	Guess: _____ Right/Wrong?
8 ... would rather watch a crime drama than a documentary. _____ _____?	Guess: _____ Right/Wrong?	Guess: _____ Right/Wrong?	Guess: _____ Right/Wrong?
9 ... _____ _____?	Guess: _____ Right/Wrong?	Guess: _____ Right/Wrong?	Guess: _____ Right/Wrong?

And now, here is the news ...

Language focus
news headlines and stories using the present perfect and past simple

Key vocabulary
news presenters:
news reader, special correspondent, sports correspondent, weather presenter;
expressions used on TV:
Welcome to ..., And now here is ...;
other vocabulary:
cloudy, crash, damage, escape, general election, glamorous, honeymoon, mask, rainy, robber, storm, vote

Skills focus
reading, writing and speaking

Multiple intelligences
linguistic, visual and kinaesthetic

Level
intermediate

Time
45 minutes

Preparation
one photocopy, cut up into cards, for each pair of students

Warm-up

❶ Ask if any students watched the TV news last night. Ask what the main stories were. Elicit other types of stories that are typically covered on the news.

❷ Ask what type of intonation is usually used for news stories. Elicit that a serious tone is used for sad or serious stories, and a more cheerful tone is used for more light-hearted stories.

Main activity

❶ Put students into pairs and give each pair the pictures and the news items.

❷ Ask students to read the stories and match them to the pictures. Encourage them not to worry if they do not understand all the words, but to try to pick out key words that may help them.

❸ Check answers by reading out each news story in turn and asking students to hold up the picture they think goes with it.

> **Answers**
> 1 c   2 e   3 a   4 g   5 d   6 f   7 b   8 h

❹ Point out that news stories usually start with the present perfect tense and then move into the past simple to explain the events. Ask students to find examples of this in the news items they have just read.

❺ Ask each pair to team up with another pair to become a group of four. Tell them to use their own ideas to finish off each news story.

❻ Tell students in each group to choose a news reader, a sports correspondent, a special correspondent (who is at the scene of a story) and a weather presenter. Tell them they are going to work together to produce their news programme.

❼ Feed in expressions for introducing the programme (*Welcome to ...*) and for switching between different presenters (*And now here is ...*).

❽ Remind students that they should use the appropriate intonation for the different news stories.

❾ Allow students time to plan their programme and rehearse, then ask each group to perform their news programme for the class. If you have a camera, you could film the groups and allow them to watch it.

❿ Ask the class to vote on the best news stories and the best performance.

Follow-up

○ For homework or in a following lesson, ask students to write their own news stories and put together their own news programme.

○ They could either use real stories from the news, by looking on the internet or in English newspapers, or they could make up their own stories for a fun version of the news.

1   Good evening and welcome to the six o'clock news.

2   An aeroplane has crashed into a mountain in Australia. The accident happened this morning. Luckily nobody was killed but

_____
_____
_____

3   A very strong storm has hit Miami in the USA. It damaged many houses, cars and trees and _____

_____
_____
_____

4   Tomorrow it will be rainy in the north of the country and cloudy in the west. The rest of the country will

_____
_____
_____

5   A bank robber has stolen one million dollars from the central bank this morning. He had a gun and was wearing a mask. He escaped by

_____
_____
_____

6   Danny Becker has done it again. He scored the only goal last night in the United versus City match. It is his 20th goal of the season. The team

_____
_____
_____

7   The American actors George Pitt and Julia Diaz have got married in Hollywood. The wedding took place yesterday. 500 people came to the glamorous party. The honeymoon is

_____
_____
_____

8   Freddo Farnes-Barnes has won the general election. 24 million people voted for him yesterday. He promises to

_____
_____
_____

Design a game show

Language focus
modal verbs for rules

Key vocabulary
contestant, disqualified, general knowledge, glass tank, honey, take part

Skills focus
reading and speaking

Multiple intelligences
linguistic and interpersonal

Level
intermediate

Time
45 minutes

Preparation
one photocopy for each student

Warm-up

❶ Ask students if they watch game shows on television. Pretend you do not know the ones they mention and ask students to explain how the games are played.

❷ Alternatively, tell students that you recently watched a game show on television that you found interesting. Describe the rules.

❸ Teach the words *contestant, take part* and *disqualified*.

Main activity

❶ Give each student an activity sheet and ask them to look at Activity 1. This consists of three short descriptions of actual game shows. Students should read the descriptions on their own first and answer the questions.

❷ Put students into pairs or groups of three. Tell them to discuss the questions and compare their ideas.

❸ Ask students to find examples in the texts of modal verbs that are used to describe rules. Write them on the board and elicit the meanings. Make sure students understand the difference between *mustn't* and *don't have to*.

> **Answers**
> Text A: … contestants have to get into … The contestants mustn't move …
> Text B: … contestants must say a series of … They mustn't make any mistakes.
> Text C: … contestants have to answer questions … they can choose any subject they like …

❹ Refer students to Activity 2 on the sheet, and explain that they are going to design their own game show. Go through the chart with them and make sure they understand everything. Students then work in their pairs or groups to plan their game show. Tell them to use the modal verbs on the board to explain the rules.

❺ Ask each group to present their game show to the class. Correct any mistakes in their use of modals.

❻ Once students have heard all the presentations, ask them to vote for the one they think is the most unusual, the most fun and the most unpleasant.

Follow-up

○ Students could bring in costumes and props, and set up scenes for their game show to photograph, and then create posters using the photographs as publicity for the show. This would be particularly appropriate at the end of term, after exams etc.

○ Alternatively students could work in groups and choose a game show from those designed in class and create a sketch acting out a scene from the show.

Activity 1 – Read and discuss

A

In this television game show, contestants have to get into a large glass tank, and they are covered from head to toe in honey. Insects are then placed on their body. The contestants mustn't move or make any sound. The first contestant to scream or run away is disqualified. The last contestant left in the tank is the winner.

B

In this television game show, contestants must say a series of tongue twisters very fast while riding a stationary bicycle. They mustn't make any mistakes. The first one to make a mistake is pushed off their bicycle and disqualified. The game continues with new tongue twisters until only one contestant – the winner – is left.

C

In this television game show, contestants have to answer questions for two minutes on a special subject. They can choose any subject they like, for example The Plays of Shakespeare. They then answer questions for two minutes on general knowledge. The winner is the contestant with the most correct answers.

1 Which game show would you like to watch most?
2 Which sounds the most difficult?
3 Which sounds like the most fun?
4 What kind of people would take part in such a game show?
5 Would you like to take part in any of these?

Activity 2 – Design your own game show

Name of the show _____

SPECIAL COSTUMES	OBJECT OF THE GAME	RULES	PRIZES

Commercial break

Language focus
the language
of advertising;
comparatives,
superlatives and
intensifiers

Key vocabulary
*high technology, historic
sites, leather, low
temperatures, luxury,
relax, smooth ride,
sparkling*

Skills focus
reading and speaking

Multiple intelligences
linguistic, interpersonal,
kinaesthetic and
mathematical

Level
intermediate

Time
45 minutes

Preparation
one photocopy, cut
up into cards, for each
group of 3 students

Warm-up

❶ Choose a commercial that is currently being shown on TV and is either very annoying or effective. Ask students what they think of it.

❷ Ask students some general questions about commercials on TV, for example:
Which TV commercials do you like/hate?
Are there too many commercials on TV?
Do commercials work? Do you buy things you see on TV ads?

❸ Elicit some examples of language used in commercials, for example: *It's the best chocolate you can buy. / Your teeth will look really white.*

❹ Write some of these superlatives and intensifiers on the board.

Main activity

❶ Put students into groups of three. Give each group a set of cards and explain that on the cards there are eight products, and 16 phrases from TV commercials advertising these products. Tell students to work in their groups and identify each product, then match the products with the advertising phrases. Tell them that in some cases there is more than one possible answer.

❷ Alternatively, if you have a class of about 30 students, you could hand one card to each student and tell them to go around the class and form groups of three, with one product and two phrases that go together. When they have formed a group of three, they will work together.

❸ Check answers, and check that students understand all the phrases.

> **Possible answers**
> Breakfast cereal: a great start to the day / full of vitamins to keep you healthy
> Pizza: extra large and extra tasty / extra cheese, mushrooms and pepperoni
> Washing powder: washes whitest / works well at low temperatures
> Toothpaste: for sparkling teeth / a great smile
> Holiday: relax in the sun / explore historic sites
> Sofa: sit back and relax in comfort / made of luxury leather
> Car: with the latest high technology / a really smooth ride
> Shampoo: leaves your hair shiny and smooth / used by top models

❹ Explain to students that they are going to create a TV commercial. Ask each group to choose one of the products from the previous activity, or allocate a product to each group to make sure that they are all doing a different one.

❺ Explain that they must use the two phrases describing their product from the previous activity, but they are free to add more descriptions of their own. Tell them they must prepare the script and plan the action for their commercial.

❻ Students work in their groups to prepare their commercials.

❼ When everyone has finished, groups can act out their commercials for the class.

Follow-up

○ Ask students to choose a popular TV commercial from their own channels and create an English version, translating the key phrases into English.

○ Students could then act out these commercials, or produce posters for the products using the key phrases.

a great start to the day	extra large and extra tasty	full of vitamins to keep you healthy	extra cheese, mushrooms and pepperoni
washes whitest	works well at low temperatures	for sparkling teeth	a great smile
relax in the sun	explore historic sites	sit back and relax in comfort	made of luxury leather
with the latest high technology	a really smooth ride	leaves your hair shiny and smooth	used by top models

Who's who in the soap?

Language focus
describing people and
talking about personal
information

Key vocabulary
*beard, character, disguise,
looks, marital status,
missing, sociable, retired,
widow, wig*

Skills focus
reading for detail

Multiple intelligences
linguistic, interpersonal
and mathematical

Level
upper intermediate

Time
30 minutes

Preparation
one photocopy for each
student

Warm-up

❶ Ask the students which soap operas they watch.

❷ Elicit the types of characters and storylines that are typically found in soap operas. This could lead to a nice discussion about popular local soaps.

Main activity

❶ Hand out the activity sheets and put students into groups of four. Explain that the grid represents seven houses on a street that features in a soap opera called *Complicated Lives*. Explain that students must use the sentences to complete the grid with information about each of the characters: their name, marital status, looks, character, job and any extra information. Refer students to the example answer, which they can use as a starting point. Teach the key vocabulary if necessary.

❷ Point out that in England, houses on one side of a street have odd numbers and on the other side of the street they have even numbers, so the house numbers on the grid will be next door to each other.

❸ Ask groups to bring their grid to you for checking when they have completed it. You could make the activity competitive, by saying that students must complete the grid as quickly as possible, and the first group to produce a correctly completed grid is the winner.

Answers

House	4	6	8	10	12	14	16
Name	David	Betty	Edna & Eric	Susan	Kevin	Bob	Hester
Marital status	single	single	married couple	widow	divorced	widower	married – husband is missing
Looks	beard	wears a wig and dark glasses	both have grey hair and glasses	glamorous	bald	muscular	long hair
Character	confident	very secretive	friendly	mysterious	quiet	sociable	sad
Job	car salesman	unemployed	retired	school teacher	policeman	car mechanic	shop keeper
Special information	in love with Susan	really Hester's husband Harry in disguise	happily married for 40 years	in love with Bob	keeping an eye on Hester; in love with Betty	in love with Hester	her husband is missing

Follow-up

○ Ask students to continue working in their groups and write a scene for four of the characters, to fit into the soap. They could act out their scenes to the class, and the class could vote for the best.

○ Alternatively, students could work in their groups and create their own soap. They could begin by deciding on their characters and the relationships between them, then move on to creating a storyline and scene.

House number	4	6	8	10	12	14	16
Name					Kevin		
Marital status							
Looks							
Character							
Job							
Special information							

Kevin, who lives at number 12, is divorced.	The old people have grey hair and both wear glasses.	The secretive woman is actually Harry, Hester's missing husband, in disguise.
The divorced man doesn't talk much.	Bob, who lives at number 14, is in love with his long-haired neighbour.	There's a shop keeper on the street.
The man in uniform is bald.	Betty, who lives at number 6, is very secretive behind those dark glasses.	The sad woman, whose husband is missing, lives at number 16.
The bald divorced man is in love with the woman who has no job.	Bob's wife died ten years ago.	The policeman, who is in love with Betty, is investigating the woman whose husband is missing.
The widow lives between the married couple and the divorced man.	The bald man lives next to the muscular man.	There's a glamorous teacher on the street.
Susan, whose husband died, is a teacher.	The policeman is investigating the disappearance of Harry.	Hester, who lives at number 16, is sad because her husband is missing.
The mysterious woman lives at number 10.	The sociable man lives between the sad woman and the quiet man.	Susan is loved by David but she's in love with Bob.
The car salesman is single.	The confident man, who lives at number 4, sells cars.	The man with a beard lives next door to the woman who wears a wig and dark glasses.
The single man who lives at number 4 has a beard.	Two people live at number 8.	The policeman lives between the teacher and the car mechanic.
The woman who lives between the single man and the married couple has never been married.	Betty wears a wig and dark glasses.	David, who lives at number 4, is in love with the woman who is love with Bob.
The woman at number 6 does not work.	Eric and Edna have been happily married for 40 years.	The friendly couple who live next door to Susan stopped working many years ago.

How much do you know about TV?

Language focus
discussing facts about
TV; agreeing and
disagreeing; the passive

Key vocabulary
*banned, broadcast,
consume, invented,
media, non-stop, plasma
television, transmission,
transmit*

Skills focus
reading and speaking

Multiple intelligences
linguistic and
interpersonal

Level
upper intermediate

Time
30 minutes

Preparation
one photocopy, cut
up into cards, for each
group of 3 or 4 students

Warm-up

❶ Brainstorm what students know about the history of television, and television around the world. Collect their ideas on the board.

❷ Either say the following or write it on the board: *Television was invented in 1823*. Ask students to say whether they think this is true or false, and to explain why they think so. Elicit several opinions and encourage students to agree and disagree with each other.

❸ Elicit expressions for agreeing and disagreeing and write these on the board, for example:
I agree with you.
I think you're right.
No, I don't agree with you.
I think you're wrong.
No, I don't think so.

Main activity

❶ Put students into groups of three or four, and explain that they are going to play a game. Tell them that they will receive a small pile of cards. They must turn the cards over one at a time, read the fact and decide if they think it is true or false.

❷ Tell students they should discuss each fact and agree or disagree with each other, but they must reach agreement as a group. They should then put the cards into two piles, one pile for the facts they think are true and one for the facts they think are false.

❸ Give each group a set of cards and allow the groups time to discuss each fact and reach agreement.

❹ Check answers with the class, and tell students to note down how many answers their group guessed correctly. The group with the most correct answers is the winner.

> **Answers**
> TRUE: 1, 3, 5, 7, 9, 11, 13, 15, 17, 19
> FALSE: 2 (Many people were involved in inventing it), 4 (it is 20,000), 6 (boys watch more), 8 (only 200), 10 (since December 1960), 12 (38 hours), 14 (69 hours and 48 minutes), 16 (a half), 18, 20

Follow-up

◯ Tell students to look again at the statements about TV and find examples of the passive. Revise the form of the passive and elicit why it is used here (it is used when the subject of the verb is not important or not known).

◯ Ask students to work in groups and devise a True/False quiz based on their own country's popular programmes and personalities. Tell them they should use passive forms in their statements where appropriate. Groups can then challenge others to play their quiz.

The word 'television' was first used at the World Fair in Paris in 1900.

1

Television was invented by one man.

2

In January 2008 a 380cm plasma television was put on the market in Japan.

3

On average, children in the US watch 10,000 TV commercials every year.

4

In 1924 John Baird was the first person to transmit moving images.

5

Today on average girls aged 10–17 watch more television than boys.

6

The first Big Brother series was broadcast in the Netherlands in 1997.

7

In 1936 there were about 20,000 television sets in use worldwide.

8

Watching television can be dangerous. In June 2008 a Norwegian woman was killed when her television exploded.

9

The world's longest running TV cookery show is *Hasta La Cocina* in Mexico, which has been broadcast each weekday since 1 December 1970. It has been presented continually by Mrs Zarate.

10

In the US and UK people watch on average 28 hours of TV per week.

11

A typical US child consumes 28 hours of media per week (TV, radio, DVDs, video games, computers).

12

On 20 July 1969, 600 million people watched the first TV transmission from the moon.

13

In September 2005 in New York Suresh Joachim broke the Guinness world record for the longest time spent watching TV. He watched non-stop for 79 hours and 48 minutes.

14

In 1996 there were a billion TV sets worldwide.

15

In 1972 a quarter of the TVs in homes were colour sets.

16

The football World Cup was first televised in 1954.

17

In 1992 televisions were banned in Mongolia.

18

In 2008 *CSI* (*Crime Scene Investigation*) was the most popular programme in the world with 84 million viewers.

19

There is one television for every person in the world.

20

TV snakes and ladders

Language focus
expressing opinions

Key vocabulary
exist, TV personality

Skills focus
speaking

Multiple intelligences
visual, kinaesthetic and linguistic

Level
upper intermediate

Time
30 minutes

Preparation
one photocopy for each group of 3 or 4 students; one photocopy of the rules for each group

Warm-up

❶ Write on the board: *Talk about a programme on TV that annoys you.* Invite students to talk about this subject. Tell them they must talk for at least 30 seconds and must give reasons for their opinions.

❷ Briefly revise language for talking about likes and dislikes, e.g. *I really like..., I love ..,. I absolutely hate ..., I can't stand ...* and also revise language for giving opinions, e.g. *I think ..., it seems to me that ..., I would say that ...*

Main activity

❶ Explain to students that they are going to play a game in which they must talk about different subjects and give their opinions.

❷ Put students into groups of three or four and hand out the activity sheets. Explain that this is a version of a traditional board game called *Snakes and Ladders*. Make sure each group has a coin, and each student has a counter.

❸ Hand out the rules and allow time for students to read them and make sure they understand everything.

❹ Students play the game in their groups.

Follow-up

○ Ask students to use the ideas they have discussed during the game to write a few paragraphs about the TV programmes they like and dislike.

○ Alternatively, they could prepare and give a short presentation on things they like and dislike on TV.

Rules for TV snakes and ladders

1 The aim of the game is to move from square 1 to 20 as quickly as possible.

2 Players take turns to flip a coin. If the coin lands on 'heads', move forward one square, and if it lands on 'tails' move two squares.

3 When players land on a square with a question, they must answer that question and speak for at least 30 seconds. Another player will time them. If they fail to speak for 30 seconds, they miss a turn.

4 If a player lands on a square with a ladder, they climb that ladder and answer the question they find at the top.

5 If they land on a snake's head, they slide down the snake all the way to its tail and answer the question they find there.

6 If a player lands on the same square a second time (e.g. if they have slid down a snake) their answer must be different the second time.

7 The first player to reach square 20 is the winner.

From *Film, TV and Music* © Cambridge University Press 2009 **PHOTOCOPIABLE**

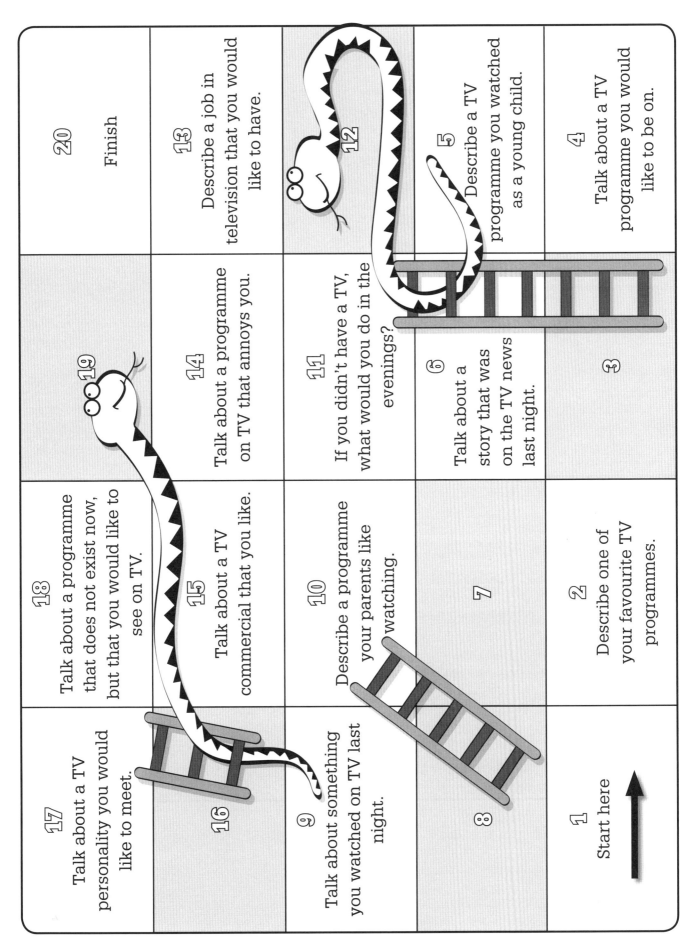

20 Finish	13 Describe a job in television that you would like to have.	12	5 Describe a TV programme you watched as a young child.	4 Talk about a TV programme you would like to be on.
19	14 Talk about a programme on TV that annoys you.	11 If you didn't have a TV, what would you do in the evenings?	6 Talk about a story that was on the TV news last night.	3
18 Talk about a programme that does not exist now, but that you would like to see on TV.	15 Talk about a TV commercial that you like.	10 Describe a programme your parents like watching.	7	2 Describe one of your favourite TV programmes.
17 Talk about a TV personality you would like to meet.	16	9 Talk about something you watched on TV last night.	8	1 Start here

Is TV bad for children?

Language focus
discussing advantages
and disadvantages

Key vocabulary
*eyesight, informed,
nutritionalist, obesity,
optician, psychologist,
sociologist*

Skills focus
reading and speaking

Multiple intelligences
linguistic and
interpersonal

Level
upper intermediate

Time
60 minutes

Preparation
one photocopy of Part A
for every 2 or 3 students;
one photocopy of Part
B, cut into role cards, for
every group of 5 students

Warm-up

1 Write up on the board *Television is bad for children.* Ask students to think about whether they agree or disagree with the statement. Brainstorm ideas and opinions with the whole class. Collect ideas on the board.

2 Briefly revise expressions for giving opinions and agreeing and disagreeing. Write useful expressions on the board e.g. *On the one hand / On the other hand, That's true, but ..., Although X is an advantage, we should also consider Y* etc.

Main activity

1 Put students into pairs or groups of three, and give each pair or group Part A of the activity sheet. Ask them to read the facts and arguments, and sort them into two groups: those that suggest TV is bad for children and those that suggest that TV is good for children.

2 Check answers, then ask students which of the facts and opinions they find most surprising, and which they find most interesting.

> **Answers**
> TV is good for children: 2, 5, 6
> TV is bad for children: 1, 3, 4

3 Ask students if they ever watch discussion programmes on the television. Elicit that such programmes have an interviewer, then a mixture of people in favour of an idea and against it.

4 Explain to students that they are going to act out a discussion programme about television. Explain that each student will get a role card and they will have to 'be' that person. One person in the group will be the interviewer.

5 Put students into groups of five. Give each group a set of role cards and ask them to share them out.

6 Ask all the students with role-play card A to come and sit together, all those with card B to sit together, etc. Tell them they have five minutes to brainstorm things they can say during the discussion. Encourage them to use the facts and arguments they looked at earlier to support their arguments.

7 The interviewers should spend this time planning what questions they want to ask, and how they will organise the discussion.

8 Put students back into their groups of five to act out the programme. You could film some of the discussions so that students can watch them later and evaluate how well they put forward their arguments.

Follow-up

○ If students are preparing for exams, ask them to write up their ideas in an essay entitled: *Watching television is harmful to children – discuss.*

○ Alternatively, you could have a class discussion in which students express their own opinions and arguments.

TV 3.4　Is TV bad for children?

A

1　Doctors say that television viewing among children is associated with irregular sleep patterns. This can make children tired and unable to concentrate.

2　A leading sociologist says that television has become an important part of children's social lives. It is one of the subjects that children talk about most often, and so it helps them to make friends.

3　Scientists tell us that TV viewing is now considered a cause of obesity. Sitting in front of a screen takes up a large part of children's lives and has replaced physical activity for many of them. Scientists warn that this will have serious consequences for their health later in life. Nutritionists agree that watching TV encourages bad eating habits.

4　Opticians say watching TV for long periods can lead to permanent eyesight damage.

5　A new study by psychologists says that families often meet up to watch TV together. It seems that TV can encourage families to spend time together and discuss things.

6　Some teachers have said that children who watch quality TV programmes about history, science and geography are much more informed about the world, and so more likely to do well at school.

B

A Doctor – agree
- TV is very bad for children's eyesight and they don't do enough exercise.
- Children need more exercise.
- Watching TV encourages children to eat junk food, which adds to weight problems.
- Watching TV can cause problems with eyesight in children.

B Teenager – disagree
- TV makes life less boring.
- You need to relax after a hard day at school.
- You can learn a lot from documentaries and science programmes.
- TV inspires you when you see famous people being interviewed.

C Parent – agree
- You never see your children because they are always in their rooms watching TV in the evening.
- They don't want to do anything with you.
- Your children pick up bad language from TV.
- They should spend more time on homework and sports.

D TV Producer – disagree
- You produce many educational programmes.
- There is a lot of TV specially designed for children and teenagers.
- Parents can guide children not to watch inappropriate programmes.
- TV is an important part of the modern world.

E Interviewer
It is your job to ask questions, make sure everyone has a chance to speak and keep everyone under control.

What happens next?

Language focus
creating a TV drama plot

Key vocabulary
glasses, revolver

Skills focus
speaking

Multiple intelligences
visual, linguistic and
interpersonal

Level
upper intermediate

Time
30 minutes

Preparation
one photocopy, cut
up into cards, for each
group of 4 students

Warm-up

❶ Ask the students which television dramas or soap operas they watch. Ask some students to tell the class what is happening at the moment in their favourite series. Elicit that the plots are often very complicated.

❷ Explain that we usually use present tenses to describe the events in a TV drama or soap opera.

Main activity

❶ Put students into groups of four. Explain that they are going to create a TV drama plot.

❷ Give each group a set of pictures. Tell students to put them in a pile face down on the table, so that everyone in the group can reach them.

❸ Explain that one at a time students will pick up a card and use the objects in the pictures to create a TV drama story. The first student starts the story, then the next student picks up a card and continues the story, and so on. Tell students they must listen carefully to other students so that they do not lose track of the plot.

❹ Tell students they can speak for as long or short a time as they wish. The aim is to incorporate each object cleverly into the plot. The student who picks the final card must try to resolve the story as best they can.

❺ Students work in their groups and create their stories.

Follow-up

○ Ask each group to work together and use the cards as prompts to tell the rest of the class the story they created. The class could vote to decide which they think is best.

○ Alternatively, groups could prepare and then act out their stories.

○ Students could also write up their stories as either a short story or a script.

What happens next?

Musical pairs

Language focus
vocabulary of musical instruments; asking and answering questions in the present simple

Key vocabulary
cello, drums, flute, guitar, harp, piano, saxophone, trombone, trumpet, violin

Skills focus
speaking

Multiple intelligences
linguistic, visual, musical and interpersonal

Level
elementary

Time
30 minutes

Preparation
one photocopy, cut up into cards, for each group of 4 students

Extra notes
The follow-up activity allows students to have some fun learning new vocabulary. Students should enjoy miming or making the sounds of instruments, and it provides an opportunity for them to consolidate the meaning of the vocabulary in a sensory way.

Warm-up

❶ Ask the class if anyone plays a musical instrument. Elicit what instrument they play, and if they enjoy it.

❷ Ask which instruments they like listening to, and again elicit some names of instruments.

Main activity

❶ Put students into groups of four and give each group a set of cards. Tell students to match the names of the instruments to the pictures. Allow students to use dictionaries if necessary. You could do this as a race if you think your students will enjoy the competitive element.

❷ Check their answers (see the layout on the sheet for answers). Drill the pronunciation of the words quite carefully, making sure that students get the correct stress, for example on *gui'tar* and *'cello*.

❸ Explain that they are going to use the cards to play a game. Ask the groups to shuffle all the cards together and then share them out within the group, without looking at them.

❹ Tell students they can now look at their own cards, but must not show them to anyone else.

❺ Explain that students must try to collect as many 'pairs' of words and pictures as possible, so for example if a student has a picture of a trumpet they must try to find a card with the word *trumpet* on it to make a pair.

❻ Explain that the way they will collect cards is by moving around the classroom and asking other students, for example:
Have you got a picture of a trumpet?
Have you got the word 'trumpet'?

Drill these questions with the class, and also check and drill the short answers:
Yes, I have / No, I haven't.

❼ Explain that students can only ask for a card if they already have one of the pair, and they can only ask other students one question at a time, then they must move on. Tell them that if they have a card someone asks them for, they must give it.

❽ Set a time limit of five minutes, then students play the game.

❾ Ask students to count up how many pairs they have collected, and get them to check with a partner that their pairs are correct. The winner is the student with the most pairs.

Follow-up

○ Tell students you are going to pretend to play an instrument and they must guess which instrument it is. Perform a mime, and make the sound of the instrument. Students should guess what you are playing.

○ Ask students in turn to volunteer to come to the front of the class and do the same thing. Tell them they can mime playing the instrument, make the sound or do both these things.

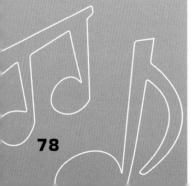

guitar		piano	
drums		violin	
trombone		cello	
trumpet		flute	
harp		saxophone	

Interview with a star

Language focus
asking and answering personal questions in the present simple and past simple

Key vocabulary
big hit, easy, favourite musician, great, instruments, meeting people, seeing new places, travelling, you're welcome

Skills focus
reading and speaking

Multiple intelligences
linguistic, mathematical, kinaesthetic and interpersonal

Level
elementary

Time
30 minutes

Preparation
one photocopy, cut up into cards, for each pair of students

Warm-up

❶ Ask students who their favourite pop stars are, and elicit some names.

❷ Tell students they are going to read an interview with an imaginary pop star called Joolie Star. The interviewer is a journalist called Toby. Ask students what questions they think the interviewer will ask.

Main activity

❶ Put students into pairs and give each pair a set of cards. Allow them time to read the cards, and explain any vocabulary they don't understand.

❷ Explain that they need to match the questions to the answers, and put them in the correct order to form the interview.

❸ Check answers. There is no fixed order for the interview, apart from the two opening questions and the closing comments (see layout on activity sheet for suggested order).

❹ Ask a pair of students to read the interview aloud and correct the pronunciation as necessary.

❺ Ask the students to work in pairs to act out the interview. They should take it in turns to be Joolie and Toby. Encourage them to be in character and read the lines with feeling.

Follow-up

○ Ask students to choose a pop star they like and work in pairs to prepare and act out an interview with them. They can use the interview with Joolie as a model and make any necessary changes.

○ Students might like to make this more realistic by first doing some research on the internet on the star they have chosen.

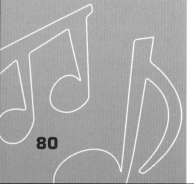

Hi Joolie! Great to meet you.	Hi Toby. It's great to meet you, too.
Can I ask you a few questions?	Yes, of course you can.
What was the name of your first big hit?	It was called 'Summer in Love'. It's a great song.
Do you write your own songs?	Yes, I do write most of them. My brother writes songs for me too.
How old were you when you started singing?	I was just four years old. All my family sing, so it was easy.
Do you like travelling around the world?	I love it. I really love meeting people everywhere and seeing new places.
Who is your favourite musician?	I really like Justin Timberlake, but I also love Madonna.
What instruments can you play?	I can play the guitar and the piano, and I also play the drums and the saxophone.
Goodbye and thanks for the interview.	You're welcome. Bye!

My song

Language focus
pronunciation and
rhyming words

Key vocabulary
*fly, glad, near, sad, set me
free*

Skills focus
listening and writing

Multiple intelligences
musical, linguistic and
interpersonal

Level
elementary

Time
45 minutes

Preparation
one photocopy for each
pair of students

Warm-up

❶ Write the following words on the board: CAT, FAT, SAT. Ask students what the words have in common (they rhyme).

❷ Ask the students if they know any other words that rhyme in English and collect some on the board.

❸ Ask students where they might find rhyming words. Elicit that songs often contain words that rhyme.

Main activity

❶ Put students into pairs and give each pair an activity sheet. Ask students to look at Activity 1. Explain that the object of this game is to find a path from the *Start* in the top left-hand corner of the maze to the *Finish* in the bottom right. They can move one square at a time, horizontally, or vertically (not diagonally), but they can only move onto squares that rhyme.

❷ Allow students a few minutes to complete the task, then check answers.

> **Answer**
> The correct route is **bear – hair – air – pair – fair – there – wear – stair – care**

❸ Refer students to Activity 2. Explain that they should complete the grid by finding words in the maze in Activity 1 which rhyme with each of the words in the grid. Do a couple of examples with the class until they understand what they have to do.

❹ Check answers.

Answers

here	high	see	friend	go
near	eye	me	end	no
dear	fly	free	send	know

❺ Refer students to Activity 3. Explain that these are two songs which students must complete. Draw attention to the different rhyming patterns: Song 1 = A–B–A–B, song 2 = A–A–B–B.

❻ Ask students to continue working in their pairs and complete the second verses of both songs. Tell them they can use words from the grid or any others they can think of.

❼ Ask students to read out their completed songs.

Follow-up

○ Students could put their lyrics to a tune and perform their songs for the class. Students could vote for the best version of the song.

○ Alternatively, for stronger classes, students could work in groups to produce their own song lyrics using the words that have been given. They can then perform their songs or write them up and display them in the classroom.

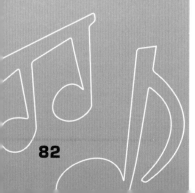

Music 1.3 My song

Activity 1

bear	here	eye	me	friend
hair	air	pair	know	no
dear	fly	fair	there	free
go	send	near	wear	stair
sat	see	high	end	**care**

Start (at bear) / **Finish** (at care)

Activity 2

here	high	see	friend	go

Activity 3

Song 1

I love you so
You set me free.
I want you to know
You are everything to me.

Don't say no
You're my best friend.

_____

_____

Song 2

When you're near
Standing here
I'm so glad
I can't be sad.

I want to fly

_____

_____

From *Film, TV and Music* © Cambridge University Press 2009 PHOTOCOPIABLE

A musical survey

Language focus
using quantifiers and talking about graphs

Key vocabulary
bar chart, can, drums, guitar, piano, pie chart, play, sing, violin

Skills focus
speaking

Multiple intelligences
linguistic, interpersonal, mathematical and kinaesthetic

Level
elementary

Time
30 minutes

Preparation
one photocopy, cut into Parts A and B, for each student

Extra notes
This activity is an example of an English Across the Curriculum task linking English and Maths. It asks students to present findings from a survey in the form of graphs, and then talk about their findings.

Warm-up

❶ Draw a simple graph on the board and elicit the word *graph*. Elicit the kinds of information that can be shown on graphs.

❷ Give each student Part A of the activity sheet. Elicit what the different graphs are called (*bar chart* and *pie chart*) and what they show.

❸ Elicit some words that are useful for presenting graphs, e.g. *Most people ..., Some people ..., A few people ..., Half the people. ..* Write these on the board.

❹ Explain that the students are going to conduct a survey on music, present their findings in graphs and then talk about their findings to the rest of the class.

Main activity

❶ Give each student Part B of the activity sheet. Refer students to the two grids and explain that they are going to carry out two surveys to find out what instruments members of the class play, and what bands and singers they like.

❷ Refer students to the first grid and elicit ideas for which instruments should be included in the survey. Make sure everyone has the same instruments on their grid. You could suggest that a 'No instrument' is included as an option, if you think that a lot of students don't play any instruments.

❸ Elicit the questions and answers that students will need to use in order to complete this part of the survey and write them on the board, e.g. *Can you play the piano / guitar etc.? Yes, I can / No, I can't.*

❹ Refer students to the second grid and again elicit ideas for which singers and bands should be included in the survey. Make sure that all students write down the same options.

❺ Elicit the questions that students will need to ask for this part of the survey and write them on the board, e.g. *Do you like Madonna / Justin Timberlake etc.? Yes, I do / No, I don't.*

❻ Divide the class into two groups, and tell one group to question members of the class about instruments, and the other to question the class about the bands they like. Allow students to mingle freely to ask the questions and fill in their grids.

❼ When they have finished, put students who have carried out the same survey into groups of three or four, and ask them to produce a graph showing their results. They can use the graphs on the activity sheet as examples. Tell them that once they have produced their graph, they must prepare some sentences to tell the class what they found. Refer them to the language on the board to help them.

❽ Groups can present their graphs and findings to the class.

Follow-up

○ Ask students what other types of information they could find out about the music tastes or skills of the class, for example who buys CDs regularly, who downloads music from the internet, who listens to music while they are doing their homework. Get students to create and carry out their own surveys and then present the findings.

○ Alternatively, students could write a short report describing their findings.

Music 1.4) A musical survey

A

Musical instruments we can play

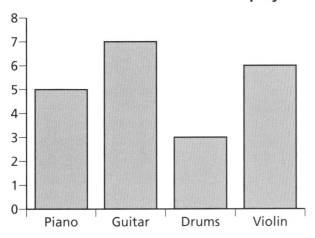

Bands and singers we like

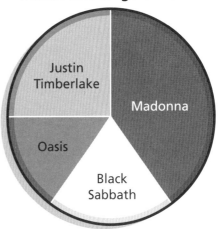

- ✂ — ✂ — — — — — — — —

B

Instrument	Number of students

Bands and singers	Number of students

My Graph

Musical record breakers

Language focus
asking and answering questions in the present simple, past simple and present perfect

Key vocabulary
date of birth, glamorous, place of birth, punk, quiet, record breaker, style, talented

Skills focus
reading for specific information and speaking

Multiple intelligences
linguistic, interpersonal and kinaesthetic

Level
elementary

Time
40 minutes

Preparation
one photocopy of Part A for each student; one reading text from Part B for each student

Warm-up

❶ Write RECORD BREAKER on the board and elicit or teach students that it refers to someone who holds a world record for being the best, the fastest, the youngest etc. person to do something.

❷ Elicit some record breakers that students know, then ask them what record breakers they think there are in the world of music. Elicit some ideas, e.g. the singer who has sold the most CDs, the band that has made the most money etc.

❸ Pre-teach the words *classical music, punk, glamorous*.

Main activity

❶ Explain that students are going to read about some musical record breakers.

❷ Give each student a copy of Part A of the activity sheet, and go through the grid as a class to make sure students understand everything. Check that students know the words for the instruments: *violin, trombone*.

❸ Divide the class into three groups. Hand out reading 1 to one group and readings 2 and 3 to the other two groups.

❹ Put students who are reading the same text into pairs. Tell them to read their text and fill in the grid with information about their musician.

❺ Explain that students are going to exchange information about the different musicians. Elicit the questions they need to ask and write them on the board:
What's his/her name? / Where was he/she born?
When did he/she start playing music? / Where does he/she live now?
What's his/her style? / What record has he/she broken?

❻ Tell students to walk around the room and find someone who has information about another musician. They should ask the questions about the musicians in order to fill in their grid.

❼ When all students have finished, check the answers with the class.

> **Answers**
>
> **Nigel Kennedy:** 28 December 1956; Brighton, England; four; Poland; not very smart, punk; sold most classical CDs ever in 1989
>
> **Vanessa Mae:** 27 October 1978; Singapore; five; London; glamorous; richest young musician in 2006
>
> **Peter Moore:** 1996; Northern Ireland; seven; Manchester, England; quiet; youngest Young Musician of the Year, 2008

Follow-up

○ Put students into pairs and ask them to prepare and act out mini interviews with one of these musicians using the facts they have.

○ Alternatively they can find out about musicians they are interested in who are record breakers and present their information about them in a following class.

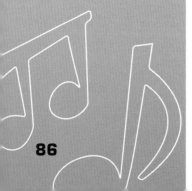

A

Record breakers			
Name			
Date of birth			
Place of birth			
Began playing music at age			
Now lives in			
Style			
Record			

✂ -

B

1

Nigel Kennedy was born in Brighton, England on 28 December 1956. He started playing the piano when he was four, but soon discovered that his real passion was for the violin. He loved jazz music. He made his first CD when he was 28. In 1989 he broke a world record. He sold the most CDs of a piece of classical music. It was a recording of Vivaldi's *The Four Seasons* – he sold two million copies!

He lives in Poland now. He enjoys jogging, and he likes watching football matches. He is a supporter of Aston Villa Football Club. He doesn't usually wear very smart clothes, and he has a punk hairstyle.

✂ -

2

Vanessa Mae was born in Singapore on 27 October 1978. Her father is Thai and her mother is Chinese. She started playing the violin at the age of five. Vanessa moved to London with her mother when she was four. She still lives there, but she also spends a lot of time travelling.

She became famous when she was still a child. She appeared on some children's TV programmes in England, playing her violin. In 2006 she broke a musical record. She became the richest young musician in the world. She is very beautiful and wears glamorous clothes.

✂ -

3

Peter Moore was born in Northern Ireland in 1996. He started playing the trombone when he was seven. He now lives in Manchester with his family, and he goes to Chetham's School of Music. He is a very talented musician. As a person, he is very quiet. He doesn't like showing his friends how good he is at music. In 2008, when he was 12 years old, he broke a musical record. He became the youngest winner of the Young Musician of the Year competition in Britain.

Musical fashions

Language focus
describing people

Key vocabulary
basic language for
describing people, plus:
*beehive, bling, braided
hair, eyeliner, motif,
spiky hair*

Skills focus
speaking and listening

Multiple intelligences
visual, linguistic and
interpersonal

Level
elementary

Time
45 minutes

Preparation
one photocopy for
each pair of students;
photos of famous pop
stars showing different
fashions and styles.
Students will also
need plain paper for
drawing on.

Warm-up

❶ Bring in (or ask your students to bring in) pictures of a few famous performers. Stick them onto the board and ask students to describe them. Encourage them to use the expressions *He's/She's got ...* and *He's/She's wearing ...*

❷ Ask students to describe any fashions they know that go with certain types of music, for example punk or heavy metal.

Main activity

❶ Put students into pairs and give each pair an activity sheet. Ask students to match the descriptive expressions with the musicians.

❷ Check their answers (see Answers below) and check or teach any vocabulary that students don't understand.

❸ Write on the board: *He/She is … He/She's got … He/She is wearing ...*
Ask students to work in their pairs and write sentences about each of the musicians, using the sentence stems on the board and the expressions on the activity sheet. Do a few examples as a class, until students understand the task, for example: *She's got long hair. He's wearing a suit.*

❹ Check answers by asking some students to read out their sentences.

> **Answers**
> **a** She's got a beehive hairstyle. She's wearing lots of eyeliner. She's thin. She's got long, dark hair.
> **b** He's wearing a suit. He's got braided hair. He's wearing lots of bling.
> **c** He's got long hair and a beard. He's wearing a T-shirt with a motif.
> **d** She's thin. She's got dyed spiky hair.

❺ Explain that now you are going to give students a picture dictation: you are going to describe a musician to them, and they are going to draw a picture of the person you are describing.

❻ Read out the following description quite slowly, then allow students time to complete their drawings.

> This woman has got long dark hair. She is wearing dark glasses and a small cap. She is thin and is wearing a small T-shirt and tight black leather trousers. She is also wearing big boots.

❼ Students can check their answers by showing each other what they have drawn.

Follow-up

○ Ask students to draw a picture of a musician or pop star, but not let anyone see their picture. Tell them it can be a real person, or an imaginary one. Working with a partner, they dictate their picture while their partner draws, and then change roles.

○ Alternatively students could find a picture in a magazine and bring it along to the following lesson. They could dictate it to the class in the same way, then other students can compare their drawing with the original.

Musical fashions

a She's ...

_____

_____

_____

b He's ...

_____

_____

_____

c He's ...

_____

_____

_____

d She's ...

_____

_____

_____

... got a beehive hairstyle.

... wearing lots of eyeliner.

... wearing a suit.

... got long, dark hair.

... wearing lots of bling.

... got braided hair.

... got long hair and a beard.

... wearing a T-shirt with a motif.

... got dyed spiky hair.

... thin.

Music crossword

Language focus
writing definitions
of general music
vocabulary

Key vocabulary
*classical, concert,
drummer, fans, flute,
folk keyboards, manager,
to record, roadie, vocalist*

Skills focus
speaking and listening

Multiple intelligences
linguistic, visual,
mathematical and
interpersonal

Level
intermediate

Time
30 minutes

Preparation
one photocopy, cut into
Parts A and B, for each
pair of students

Extra notes
Have dictionaries
available for students to
use.

Warm-up

❶ Put students into pairs and allocate four minutes for them to brainstorm as much vocabulary as they can think of connected to music.

❷ Put pairs together to form groups of four, and tell them to compare their lists.

Main activity

❶ Write the word VIOLIN on the board and ask students to describe it without naming it, for example: *It's a musical instrument, we often hear it in classical music, you play it with your hands, you put it on your shoulder to play it*, etc.

❷ Divide the class into two groups and give a copy of crossword A to each student in one group, and a copy of crossword B to each student in the other group. Explain that they each have half a crossword, and they are going to complete it by exchanging clues with a student from the other group.

❸ Put students into groups of three or four students, all with the same crossword. Explain that they must prepare definitions or clues for the words in their crossword, which they will exchange with a student from the other group.

❹ Go around and monitor, and check students' definitions as they write them.

❺ When students have finished and you have checked all their definitions, ask them to pair up with a student from the other group.

❻ Explain that they should now take it in turns to read out clues for the words they have, so that their partner can guess the words and write them into their crossword. Teach *one across, two down* etc.

❼ Students can check their answers by looking at their partner's crossword.

Follow-up

⭘ Ask students to continue working in their pairs and categorise the words that appeared in the crosswords under the following headings: *Types of music, People, Instruments, Events*. They could then use dictionaries to add two or three more words to each category.

⭘ Alternatively, they could work in pairs to think of other words to do with music and write definitions for them. They could then design their own crosswords, using a website to make the puzzles, for example: http://puzzlemaker.school.discovery.com

⭘ They can bring their crosswords to the next class and give them to other students to do.

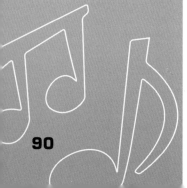

A

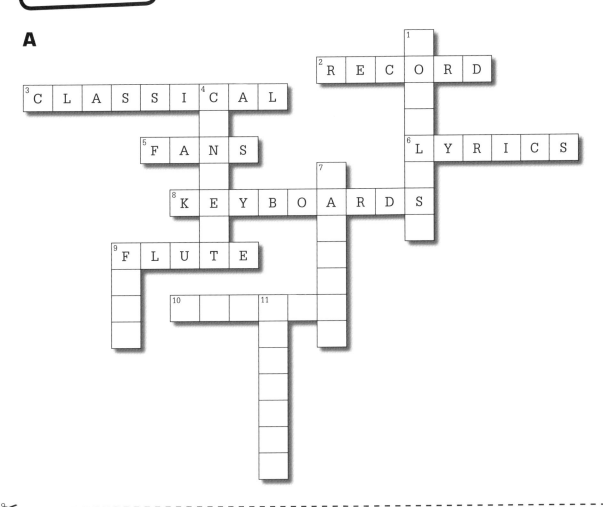

B

Interview with a star

Language focus
asking and answering questions about a career in music

Key vocabulary
ambition, band member, hit

Skills focus
writing and speaking

Multiple intelligences
linguistic and interpersonal

Level
intermediate

Time
40 minutes

Preparation
one photocopy, cut into Parts A and B, for each pair of students

Warm-up

❶ Ask students who their favourite musicians and bands are, and elicit a few names.

❷ Ask students what they know about their favourite bands and musicians. Ask them some questions about the band or musician, for example when they first started playing or when they had their first hit.

Main activity

❶ Explain to the class that they are going to role play an interview between a band member and a journalist. Divide the class into two halves, and tell one half that they will be the band members and the other half that they will be journalists.

❷ Give each band member Part A of the activity sheet, and each journalist Part B of the activity sheet.

❸ Put students into groups of four, with four journalists working together and four band members working together.

❹ Tell the students who are band members that they should invent information about themselves and fill in the sheets.

❺ Tell the students who are journalists that they should prepare questions based on the prompts on the sheet.

❻ Allow about five minutes for students to complete these tasks. Monitor around the class, and check that the journalists have formed all their questions correctly.

❼ Put students into pairs of one band member and one journalist. Tell them they should now plan and rehearse their interview. Encourage them to get into character rather than just read out the information they have prepared.

❽ When they are ready, invite pairs to come to the front of the class and act out their interviews. If possible, you could film the interviews and allow students to watch them afterwards.

Follow-up

○ Ask students to continue working in their pairs and write an article for a music magazine based on the interview.

○ Alternatively, students could prepare information about real musicians and then act out interviews with them.

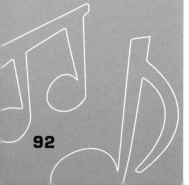

Music 2.2 Interview with a star

A

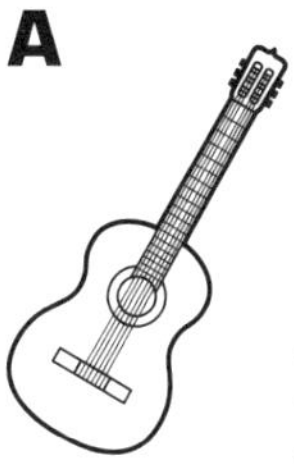

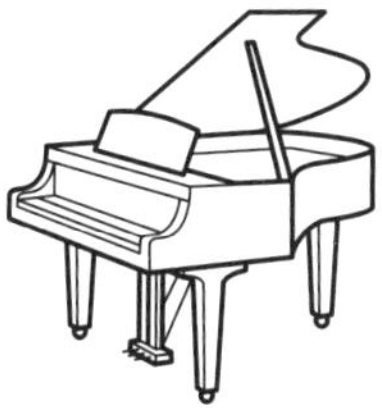

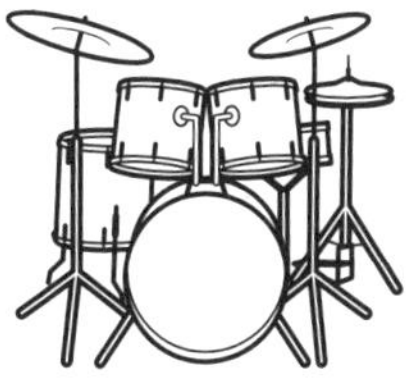

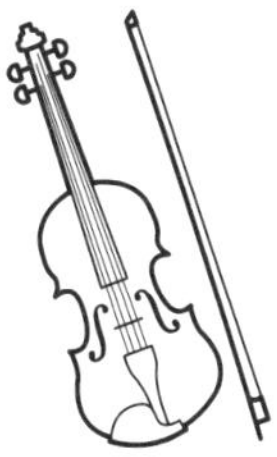

My band

Name of band ______________________

Instrument I play ______________________

Type of music we play ______________________

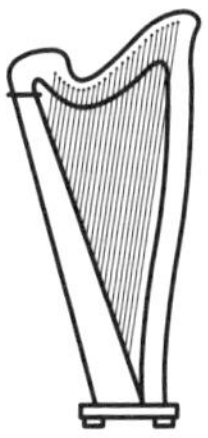

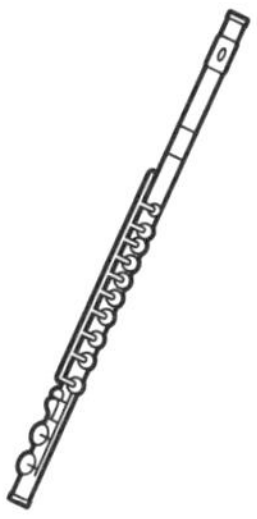

Other members of the band ______________________

Began playing in ______________________

First hit in ______________________

Name of first hit ______________________

Next concert ______________________

Best country I've visited ______________________

Ambitions ______________________

An interesting fact about the band ______________________

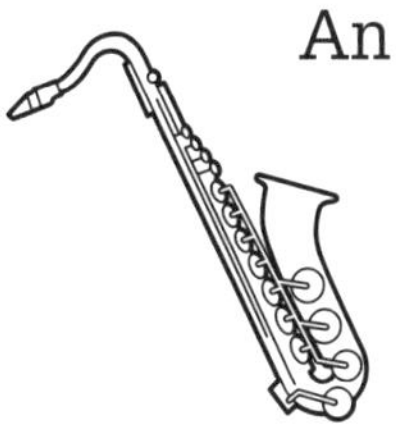

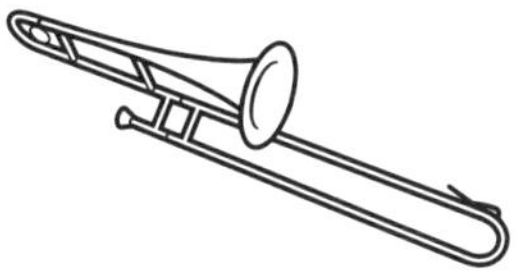

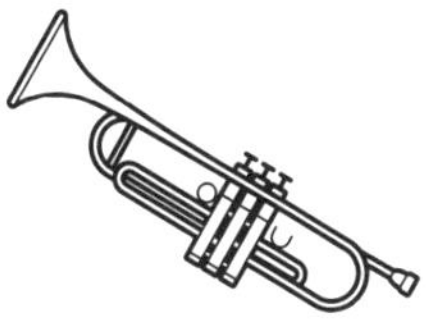

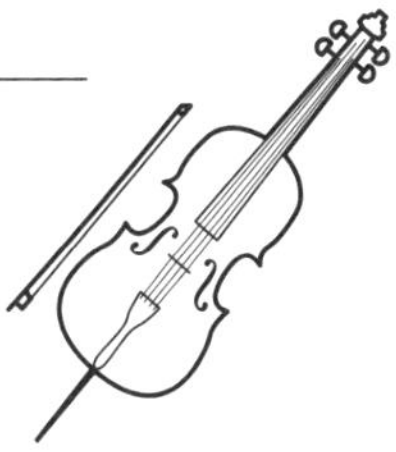

B

Questions to ask the band member

name / band: ______________________?

instrument / you / play ______________________?

type of music / you / play ______________________?

who / else / in / the band ______________________?

when / begin / playing ______________________?

when / first / hit ______________________?

what / name / first hit ______________________?

when / next / concert ______________________?

what / best country / you / visit ______________________?

what / your / ambitions ______________________?

tell me / one / interesting fact / about / the band ______________________?

Beat the clock!

Language focus
talking and giving opinions about music

Key vocabulary
background music, beach, lift, lyrics, national anthem, orchestra, TV commercial

Skills focus
speaking

Multiple intelligences
linguistic and interpersonal

Level
intermediate

Time
30 minutes

Preparation
one photocopy, cut up into cards, for each group of 4 to 6 students; one photocopy of the rules for each group

Extra notes
The rules say that players must speak for 30 seconds. This amount of time can be increased or decreased according to the ability of individual classes.

Warm-up

❶ Write on the board MY FAVOURITE BAND. Invite students to try to talk for 30 seconds on this subject.

❷ Explain that one of the skills of talking is being able to sustain conversation and not just speak in single words or phrases, and that it is not always necessary to focus on grammatical accuracy, especially in real-life situations.

Main activity

❶ Explain to students that they are going to play a speaking game, in which they must try to talk for at least 30 seconds on one subject without pausing. It doesn't matter if grammar is not perfect, as long as people can understand what they are saying.

❷ Pre-teach the key vocabulary.

❸ Elicit some expressions that students can use as 'fillers' if they cannot think of anything to say, e.g. *In my opinion ..., As I said before ... .*

❹ Put students into groups of four to six students and give each group a set of cards.

❺ Hand out a copy of the rules and allow students time to read them, or go through them as a class.

❻ Students play the game in their groups.

Follow-up

○ Ask students to choose one of the topics and write a paragraph on that subject, this time focusing on grammatical accuracy as well as interesting ideas.

○ Alternatively students can create their own version of the game by writing the cue cards. This could be restricted to a particular topic or could be totally free.

Rules for Beat the clock!

1 Each player in turn picks up a card.

2 They can think for a few seconds before they start to speak.

3 When they start to speak, another student must time them and see if they can speak for 30 seconds.

4 If they speak for 30 seconds successfully, without pausing too much, they get a point.

5 The winner is the player with the most points at the end of the game.

From *Film, TV and Music* © Cambridge University Press 2009 **PHOTOCOPIABLE**

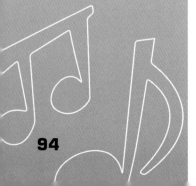

Music 2.3 Beat the clock!

Music that is played in lifts and shops		The music I'd like to have at my birthday party	
My favourite songs		My favourite singers	
Music that I really dislike		The national anthem of my country	
Background music in films		Classical music	
Concerts I have been to		Music from my country	
Orchestras		Music on the radio	
Music that reminds me of when I was a small child		Music my parents / grandparents like	
Music that makes me cry		My favourite lyrics	
Music for dancing		The first CD I ever bought	
Music in TV commercials		Music for the beach	
My favourite instruments		Music for the car	

Hip hop quiz

Language focus
vocabulary of music and
music culture

Key vocabulary
*Djing, dynamic, graffiti,
jewellery, lifestyle,
scratching, showy, style,
vinyl*

Skills focus
reading

Multiple intelligences
kinaesthetic, musical
and interpersonal

Level
intermediate

Time
30 minutes

Preparation
one photocopy of the
quiz for each group of 4
students; one photocopy
of the reading strips, cut
up, for the whole class.
Before the class, stick the
reading strips to walls,
ideally in the corridor
outside the classroom,
or in the classroom in
places that students
cannot see from their
seats.

Warm-up

❶ Ask students what their favourite type of music is. Brainstorm some different
types of music, for example pop, indie, jazz, rap. Write the words on the board.

❷ Ask students to give examples of artists or groups that play these types of music.

❸ Ask students if there are other things associated with these types of music, for
example particular styles of clothing, hairstyles etc.

Main activity

❶ Tell the students that they are going to do a quiz about rap and hip hop. Tell
them not to worry if they don't know much about this type of music, as they will
have the chance to find out.

❷ Tell them that outside the classroom in the corridor are five strips of paper with
useful information to help them do the quiz, and you will tell them when they
can go and find it.

❸ Put students into groups of four and give each group a copy of the quiz. Tell
students to spend a few minutes trying to answer as many questions as they
can.

❹ Explain that when you say 'Go', students will be able to go and find the
information in the corridor. Tell them that only one member of each group can
go out at a time, then they must come back and report to the group what they
have learned.

❺ Start the activity by saying *Go!*

❻ Stop the activity after about six or seven minutes. Tell students that if they have
not managed to find all the answers, they will have to guess the remaining ones.

❼ Check the answers with the class and see which group got the most answers
right.

Answers
1 d   2 b   3 b   4 a   5 b   6 b   7 b   8 c

Follow-up

◯ Explain to students that they are going to prepare a similar quiz to test their
classmates on a different type of music. Suggest that they choose a type of
music they know a lot about, and follow the format of the hip hop quiz.

◯ Students can work in groups, finding information on the internet or in
magazines. If there are no computers at school, students can do this for
homework.

◯ Either make copies of the quizzes, or they could be read aloud.

The hip hop quiz

1 Hip hop is not just music, it's also
   a. DJing
   b. breakdancing
   c. graffiti
   d. all the above

2 Hip hop began in
   a. London
   b. New York
   c. Los Angeles

3 Hip hop started in
   a. the 1960s
   b. the 1970s
   c. the 1980s

4 Which one of these artists is not a rapper?
   a. Madonna
   b. Eminem
   c. Kanye West

5 Bling is part of hip hop culture. What is it?
   a. a type of song
   b. expensive jewellery, cars and clothes
   c. a female rapper

6 B-boying means
   a. boys dancing with girls
   b. boys dancing to hip hop music
   c. girls dancing to hip hop music

7 Scratching means
   a. writing graffiti on walls
   b. moving vinyl records when DJing
   c. writing rap music

8 RAP means:
   a. Real American People
   b. Red Angry Party
   c. Rhythmic American Poetry

✂ -
✂ -

Hip hop culture began in the Bronx district in New York City.

The four elements of hip hop are rapping, breakdancing, graffiti and DJing. DJing is audio mixing (mixing parts of different songs together) and scratching (moving vinyl records to make distinctive scratching sounds).

The bling bling lifestyle associated with hip hop focuses on expensive and showy jewellery, cars and clothes.

Hip hop began in the 1970s.

B-boying (or B-girling, for women) is also known as breakdancing. It is a dynamic style of street dancing.

An overnight success

Language focus
discussing options and
making decisions

Key vocabulary
*busking, career, cruise
ship, download music,
executive, inspiration,
manager, a musical, sign
a contract, solo artist,
talent show, world tour*

Skills focus
reading and speaking

Multiple intelligences
linguistic and
interpersonal

Level
intermediate

Time
45 minutes

Preparation
one photocopy of
activity sheets A and B,
cut up into cards, for
each group of 3 or 4
students

Warm-up

❶ Write OVERNIGHT SUCCESS on the board. Explain that this term is often used in the music business to mean that someone becomes famous and successful very quickly. Ask students if they think people can become a success overnight.

❷ Ask students to work in small groups and brainstorm what they think people must do and what choices they must make in order to become successful in the music business, for example learn to play an instrument, meet the right people etc. Elicit ideas from groups and write them up on the board focusing on any new language that comes up.

Main activity

❶ Explain to students that they are going to work in groups and do a reading maze to see if they become a successful pop star or not. Explain that this means they must read a series of cards which describe situations. For each one they must make a decision. Tell them they must discuss each card, and reach a decision as a group. The decision they make will determine which card they get next, and they should follow the instructions on the cards. Tell students they will continue reading the cards and making decisions until they discover whether they have been a success or a failure.

❷ Put students into groups of three or four. Give a set of cards to one student in each group, and tell them not to look at them until you tell them to. Explain that for each card you will allow them three minutes to talk and reach a decision, then you will tell them to find their next card.

❸ Tell the students to find card number 1, read it and discuss it.

❹ Time three minutes, then tell students to find the next card for their group.

❺ Continue in this way until students reach the end of the maze. Find out which of the groups made it to be stars.

Follow-up

○ Ask students to write a biography of the fictitious musician they created, saying how their career developed, based on ideas from the reading maze.

○ Alternatively, students could use ideas from the reading maze to prepare and act out interviews with fictitious musicians.

○ If students are interested in particular musicians, they could research information about how their careers developed and how they achieved success. They could report back to the class.

A

1
You are 14 years old. Your parents give you a guitar for your birthday.
- You find it too difficult to learn, so you give the guitar to your younger brother = go to card 2
- You love it and you're good = go to card 3

2
Your brother is a great guitarist and forms a band. He asks you to join.
- You sing backing vocals for him = go to card 17
- You decide to be his manager = go to card 18

3
- After a year, you decide to form a band with three classmates = go to card 4
- You want to be a solo artist. You continue to practise alone in your bedroom = go to card 5

4
- Your band is good and you write some songs together = go to card 6
- You parents complain that your guitar playing is too loud, so you change to playing a violin = go to card 7

5
A famous rock star driving by your house hears your music. She asks you to join her band.
- What a great opportunity. Of course you accept = go to card 19
- You don't like her music, so you say no = go to card 20

6
You are asked to play in a local club.
- You think it is too early to play in front of an audience = go to card 8
- You are so excited and agree = go to card 9

7
A very good choice. Violins become very popular and you have a special way of playing which a lot of people like.
- You record a CD of violin pop music with your band = go to card 15
- You go solo and write unusual rap/folk violin songs = go to card 16

8
You miss a good chance but instead you
- decide to try your luck and enter a TV talent show = go to card 23
- you practise at home every night = go to card 5

9
You are great and a record company asks you to sign a contract with them.
- You say no, because it's better to be independent = go to card 10
- You sign = go to card 11

10
Without the record company, you have no money and can't make CDs.

Your story ends here.

11
Your first album goes to number one in the charts.
- You decide to leave the music business and become a film star = go to card 12
- You love the success, the fame, the money too much = go to card 13
- You decide to start work on your second album = go to card 14

12
You are offered a part in a Hollywood musical (a film with songs in).
- You accept. It's a good way to start in films = go to card 31
- You only want to act now. You demand the star role in the new James Bond film = go to card 32

13
You go to too many parties and become lazy and fat. What a waste. Your music career is over.

14
You have no ideas for songs and give up trying to write new ones.
- You steal some ideas from other artists = go to card 33
- You decide to go on holiday to get inspiration = go to card 29

15
The band is a great success and you are a star – for a year. Violin pop goes out of fashion.

16
Your songs are too strange and nobody buys your music, but your friends and parents like your songs so you play for them sometimes and decide to go to university.

17
Your singing is terrible and your brother throws you out of the band.
- You decide to have singing lessons = go to card 24
- You start to learn to play the drums = go to card 25

18
Your brother's band is a great success. But you still want to be on the stage.
- Your brother asks you to be his manager and lets you sing backing vocals sometimes = go to card 34
- You decide to enter a TV talent show = go to card 23

B

You go on tour with her band and do very well. She says you are a great guitarist.
- You like the life with her band and decide to stay = go to card 21
- You think it's now time to go solo and so you leave her band = go to card 22

19

Good choice. She is arrested soon after with all her band for stealing other musicians' songs.
- You send a CD of your music to a record company = go to card 11
- You post your songs on the internet = go to card 28

20

You go on a world tour. On a visit to Africa you fall in love with African music.
- You decide to stay in Africa and join a local band = go to card 30
- You go home and form a new band and write songs with African rhythms = go to card 22

21

Good choice. You are very successful and have the chance to make an album.
- You make the album = go to card 11
- You decide to have a holiday first. It's been a busy year! = go to card 29

22

You do quite well on the talent show and are offered a job playing on cruise ships (holiday ships).
- No way. You go back to practising in your bedroom = go to card 5
- It's a job so you say yes to a one-year contract = go to card 27

23

Your teacher is excellent and your singing gets better and better. You sing at a local concert and a music company executive hears you and offers you a contract.
- You are not sure, so say no = go to card 10
- You sign the contract = go to card 11

24

You are very good at the drums.
- You practise every evening at home = go to card 5
- The neighbours complain and call the police = go to card 26

25

You decide that the music business is just too hard and you must study for school exams. You will try again in a few years.

26

The cruise ship is full of old people who don't like modern music. You give up on the music business and go home and back to school.

27

The internet makes you famous. Millions of people download your music. You are a huge success – congratulations.

28

You go on holiday to an island far away and enjoy the quiet life there. You realise the music business is too hard. But you still play your songs on the beach for the local children.

29

Your band is a huge success and you go on a world tour. You play in your home town and all your family and friends come to hear you. You are so happy. It was the right choice.

30

Musicals are popular again. You made a good choice. You are a great success and very happy.

31

You were too arrogant. No one likes you any more. Your career is finished.

32

Your fans don't like this and your record company drops you. You have no money.
- You take a job playing music on a cruise ship = go to card 27
- You start busking (playing music) in the streets = go to card 35

33

You are having fun and you have a good job. Life is good.

34

Meeting people on the streets gives you inspiration and you write some songs.
- You post them on the internet = go to card 28
- You go back to your record company and play your new songs to them = go to card 36

35

The music business is tough. The music company is not interested. It looks like your career is over.

36

Boy band or heavy metal?

Language focus
reading descriptions of different types of bands

Key vocabulary
adjectives: *choreographed, elaborate, extreme, mainstream, outrageous*
nouns: *antics, audition, image, sequence*

Skills focus
reading and speaking

Multiple intelligences
linguistic and interpersonal

Level
upper intermediate

Time
40 minutes

Preparation
one photocopy of activity sheet A or activity sheet B for each student

Warm-up

❶ Ask students what bands they like. Ask what kind of bands they are.

❷ Collect some names of different styles of music and types of bands on the board. Make sure you elicit the words *boy band* and *heavy metal band*.

Main activity

❶ Explain to students that they are going to read a text about either a boy band or a heavy metal band. Divide the class into two groups, and give out activity sheet A to students in one group and activity sheet B to students in the other group.

❷ Within each group, put students into pairs and tell them to work together to read their text and answer the questions about their text.

❸ Monitor, and check the answers of each pair, but do not do a whole class check at this stage.

> **Answers**
> **boy bands**
> 1   It's a type of pop group with three or four young male singers.
> 2   It is often put together by a talent manager or record company.
> 3   They can sing and dance.
> 4   They attract young teenage girls.
>
> **heavy metal bands**
> 1   It originated in the United Kingdom and the United States.
> 2   They usually have long hair, wear outrageous clothes, and behave in extreme ways on stage.
> 3   They are often about violent subjects.
> 4   Their fans often look like the band members, with long hair, beards, jeans and T-shirts with the band's picture on.

❹ Still in their pairs, tell students to look at the questions about the other type of band and predict the answers.

❺ Arrange students in pairs with one from group A and one from group B. Tell them to ask each other the questions they have predicted the answers to, and check whether their predictions were correct.

❻ Tell students to discuss in their pairs which of the two types of band they prefer and why.

Follow-up

○ Put students into groups of four or five and tell them to imagine they are going to form a band.

○ Tell them they should decide on a name for their band, the fashion style they will adopt, the type of music they will play, the name of their first album etc.

○ Students can present their bands to the class.

A

Boy bands

A boy band is a type of pop group which typically has three or four young male singers. The members of the band generally dance as well as sing, often performing very elaborate dance sequences which have been carefully choreographed to fit their music. A boy band generally follows mainstream music trends, and the members will change their appearance to adapt to new fashions. Their shows are usually energetic and exciting to watch. Although they are called 'bands', members of boy bands do not usually play musical instruments. They are often put together by talent managers or record companies who audition young singers and choose them for their appearance and dancing skills as well as for their singing ability. For this reason, boy bands are often criticised for being manufactured products. Famous boy bands are Backstreet Boys and Take That. Their audience is generally teenagers, especially young teenagers, and they are particularly popular with young girls.

Questions about boy bands

1 What exactly is a boy band?

_____

2 How is a boy band usually created?

_____

3 What skills do boy band members often have?

_____

4 What kind of audience do boy bands attract?

_____

Questions about heavy metal bands

Questions	Your prediction / guess	The real answer
1 Where did heavy metal originate?		
2 What kind of image do heavy metal bands have?		
3 What are the song lyrics like?		
4 What are their fans like?		

B

Heavy metal bands

Heavy metal bands have been around since the late 1960s.
They originated mainly in the United Kingdom and the
United States, and have their musical roots in blues-rock and
psychedelic music. Two of the most famous bands, who are
still playing after many years, are Iron Maiden and Black
Sabbath. Many of the bands were formed by school friends
who started playing music together in their family's garage
for fun. Bands are usually made up of drums and guitars,
and possibly a keyboard. A heavy metal band is not just
about music but also about image. Band members usually have very
long hair, wear outrageous clothes and behave in extreme ways on stage. The songs
are far from romantic, and are often about violent subjects. The music is loud, and concerts can be
unpredictable, with the musicians performing strange antics on the stage. Their fans are very loyal and
often look very much like the band with long hair, beards, jeans and T-shirts with the band's picture on.

Questions about heavy metal bands

1   Where did heavy metal originate?

   _____

2   What kind of image do heavy metal bands have?

   _____

3   What are the song lyrics like?

   _____

4   What are their fans like?

   _____

Questions about boy bands

Questions	Your prediction / guess	The real answer
1 What exactly is a boy band?		
2 How is a boy band usually created?		
3 What skills do boy band members often have?		
4 What kind of audience do boy bands attract?		

Music spiral

Language focus
expressing ideas and
opinions about music

Key vocabulary
*background music,
canned music,
concentrate*

Skills focus
speaking

Multiple intelligences
kinaesthetic and
linguistic

Level
upper intermediate

Time
30 minutes

Preparation
one photocopy for each
group of 3 or 4 students;
one photocopy of the
rules for each group;
background music to
play at the beginning of
the lesson; each group
will also need a coin to
flip

Warm-up

❶ Play some background music while students enter the classroom and settle down. Then ask if students enjoy having music in the background in their lives.

❷ After some general discussion invite individual students to speak for a whole minute about this topic. Encourage fluency and a free flow of ideas.

Main activity

❶ Explain to students that they are going to play a speaking game. Put students into groups of three or four and give each group an activity sheet.

❷ Allow students time to read the questions and topics on the spiral, and teach the key vocabulary. Explain that before they play the game they must fill in the blanks on the spiral with their own questions or topics. Allow students time to do this in their groups. If they are struggling to think of ideas, elicit some from the whole class and write them on the board.

❸ Hand out the rules of the game, and allow students time to read them, or go through them as a class.

❹ Students play the game in their groups.

Follow-up

⭕ Get feedback from the groups about which topics were the most interesting. Choose one of these topics and hand out a blank sheet of paper to each student. Ask each student to work independently and write one sentence on this topic at the top of the page. They then pass their paper to the student next to them (so papers circulate around the class). The next student reads what is written and then continues the paragraph so it is connected and logical. Continue this for about four or five sentences asking the final time for students to finish off their paragraphs.

⭕ Pin the paragraphs around the room and ask students to get up and read them, or pass them around so students can read them. Ask students to nominate which paragraphs were the best written and why.

⭕ Alternatively, you could ask students to choose the topic on the spiral they found most interesting and write a paragraph about it for homework.

Rules for Music spiral

1 Players start the game on the *Start* square.

2 Take it in turns to flip a coin. Move forward one square for 'heads', and two for 'tails'. The question or topic you land on is the one you must talk about.

3 You can think for a few seconds before you start to speak.

4 When you start to speak, another student must time you and see if you can speak for 60 seconds.

5 If you speak for 60 seconds successfully, without pausing too much, you get a point.

6 The winner is the player with the most points at the end of the game.

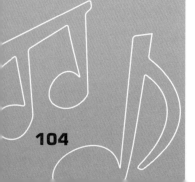

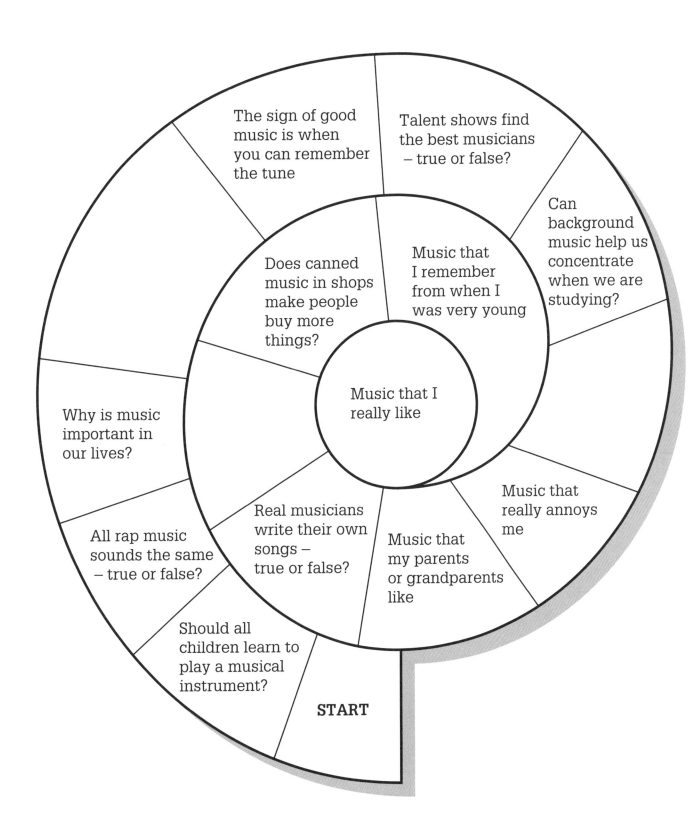

The sign of good music is when you can remember the tune

Talent shows find the best musicians – true or false?

Can background music help us concentrate when we are studying?

Does canned music in shops make people buy more things?

Music that I remember from when I was very young

Music that I really like

Why is music important in our lives?

Music that really annoys me

All rap music sounds the same – true or false?

Real musicians write their own songs – true or false?

Music that my parents or grandparents like

Should all children learn to play a musical instrument?

START

Song lyrics

Language focus
rhyme, rhythm, stress
and intonation

Key vocabulary
*brilliant, disaster,
ignorance, subway, weary*

Skills focus
reading and writing

Multiple intelligences
musical, linguistic and
interpersonal

Level
upper intermediate

Time
30 minutes

Preparation
one photocopy, cut into
Parts A and B, for each
student

Warm-up

❶ Write up the following song lyrics on the board, or have them ready on an OHT:

I see trees of green, red roses too
I see them bloom for me and you
And I think to myself what a wonderful world.

I see skies of blue and clouds of white
The bright blessed day, the dark sacred night
And I think to myself what a wonderful world.

❷ Ask students if they know where the words come from. Elicit or explain that they are song lyrics. Ask what features the words have that are typical of song lyrics. Elicit that they have rhythm, rhyme and repetition. You could read the lyrics aloud to help students to see these patterns, or get them to count the syllables in each line and identify the patterns.

Main activity

❶ Give each student Part A of the activity sheets and explain that the words on the sheet are the beginnings of four songs. Ask the students to read through them quickly and to say if they recognise the lyrics or have any idea about who the artist is or what kind of song it is. Accept all suggestions to encourage as much participation as possible.

❷ Give students the information about the songs if they are interested.

> **Answers**
> A *Until the end of time*, Justin Timberlake
> B *Careless Whisper*, George Michael
> C *I will always love you*, Whitney Houston
> D *You're beautiful*, James Blunt

❸ Put students into groups of four, and ask them to work together to complete the four tasks at the bottom of the sheet.

❹ Give out Part B of the activity sheet so that students can compare their verses with the actual ones. Suggest that students might like to listen to the songs on the internet when they get home.

Follow-up

○ Ask students for homework to choose an English song whose lyrics they particularly like and bring a CD of the song to the next lesson.

○ In class, invite students to present their songs explaining why they like the lyrics and playing the song for everyone to hear. If possible make copies of the lyrics for all the students to have.

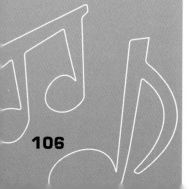

A

A
Woke up this morning
Heard the TV sayin' something
'Bout disaster in the world and
It made me wonder where I'm going
There's so much darkness in the world
But I see beauty left in you girl
And what you give me lets me know
That I'll be alright

B
Time can never mend the careless whispers of a good friend
To the heart and mind, ignorance is kind
There's no comfort in the truth
Pain is all you'll find

C
If I should stay
I would only be in your way
So I'll go but I know
I'll think of you every step of the way
And I will always love you …

D
My life is brilliant
My love is pure
I saw an angel
Of that I'm sure
She smiled at me on the subway
She was with another man
But I won't lose no sleep on that
'Cause I've got a plan

1   Read the opening lyrics. What do you think the song is about? How do you think each one continues?

2   Discuss with your groups what style of music you think goes with each song. Explain your choices.

3   Working individually, rank the lyrics – number 1, which you like best, to number 4, which you like least. Compare your thoughts with the other students in your group and explain your choices.

4   With a partner, choose one song and write a possible next verse for the song. Keep it in the same style.

✂ -

B

A
Cause if your love is all I had in this life
Well that would be enough until the end of time
So rest your weary heart and relax your mind
Cause I'm gonna love you girl until the end of time

B
I feel so unsure
As I take your hand and lead you to the dance floor
As the music dies, something in your eyes
Calls to mind the silver screen
And all its sad goodbyes
I'm never gonna dance again
Guilty feet have got no rhythm
Though it's easy to pretend
I know you're not a fool

C
Bittersweet memories
That is all I'm taking with me
So goodbye
Please don't cry
We both know I'm not what you need

D
You're beautiful. You're beautiful
You're beautiful, it's true
I saw your face in a crowded place
And I don't know what to do
'Cause I'll never be with you

Musical jobs

Language focus
writing a job advert and job application

Key vocabulary
personal qualities, e.g. *ambitious, dedicated;* vocabulary of the music industry: *artist, aspect, challenging, develop, erupt, a good ear, mix, press coverage, reviews, route*

Skills focus
reading and writing

Multiple intelligences
linguistic and interpersonal

Level
upper intermediate

Time
60 minutes

Preparation
one photocopy for each student

Extra notes
A number of formal examinations require students to write formal or semi-formal letters. This activity may fit in well to this kind of practice and provide a context for it.

Warm-up

❶ Ask students what jobs they know about in the music industry. Brainstorm different kinds of jobs as a class, and write them on the board.

❷ Ask students to consider what skills are important for different jobs, for example a roadie must be strong and must love music.

❸ Elicit words describing qualities a person has, for example *organised, dedicated, ambitious* and *hard-working.* Write these on the board and leave them there, as they will be used later.

Main activity

❶ Give each student an activity sheet. Ask students to work in pairs and complete the matching exercise in Activity 1.

> **Answers**
> 1 Tour Manager
> 2 Sound Engineer
> 3 Artist's Manager
> 4 Music Journalist
> 5 PR/Promotions Person

❷ Put students into pairs and ask them to discuss which of these jobs in the music industry they find most appealing.

❸ Ask students to continue working in their pairs and look at the job advertisement in Activity 2. Explain the word résumé if necessary. Ask them if they would like to apply for this job. Allow them a minute or two to discuss this in their pairs.

❹ Tell students that they are now going to write an advertisement for one of the jobs they have just read about, or any other job in the music industry. Tell students to work individually, and use the advertisement in Activity 2 as a model for their own advertisement.

❺ While students are working, monitor and correct any mistakes.

❻ When students have finished, pin their advertisements around the classroom and invite students to walk around in their pairs and choose one that appeals to them most.

❼ Tell students they are now going to write a letter of application for the job they have chosen. Refer students to the expressions on the board used to describe qualities, and revise expressions that are used in formal letters, e.g. *I am writing in response to your advertisement … .* You could plan and write one application letter as a class, to give students a model to work from.

❽ When students are ready to write, tell them to use their imaginations and try to create a perfect application letter.

Follow-up

○ Elicit from the whole class the kinds of questions that are asked in job interviews. Write these on the board.

○ Put students into pairs and tell them to show their partner their letter of application.

○ Allow students a few minutes to prepare their questions, then students can work in pairs and role play the job interviews for the jobs they have applied for.

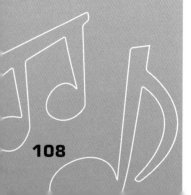

Activity 1

1 This person handles all the details of travel, from deciding the route of the tour bus to making sure that the artist is in the best condition for performing when they arrive. It's a challenging and tiring job but worth it when the artist walks onto the stage and the audience erupts with excitement.

2 This person's job is to get the best possible sound from a recording. They must know a lot about music and the technology needed to record and mix sounds.

3 This person first has to find musical talent, develop the artist, negotiate a deal with a record company and is then involved with every aspect of presenting the artist including choosing producers for their albums, organising lighting for shows and even hair and make-up.

4 This person writes news stories about artists, reviews of their concerts and albums as well as interviews with them. They have to know the music industry very well and have a good ear for what the public likes. They are also expected to travel a lot.

5 This person controls press coverage of the artist. They get journalists to listen to the artist's music and send information to the press. It is their job to make the artist a success.

Music Journalist   **Artist's Manager**   **Sound Engineer**

Public Relations/Promotions Person   **Tour Manager**

Activity 2

Music Director (Los Angeles)

Minimum Education: None
Job Type: Full Time

Candidate must have a passion for music, experience of the music industry, and experience working with Promotions/ Marketing and the Web.

Please send résumé and programming/music philosophy to ....

Your job advertisement

The big event

Language focus
negotiating and
planning a music event

Key vocabulary
*camping, charity,
costumes, exotic, floats,
parade, slogan, stalls*

Skills focus
speaking

Multiple intelligences
linguistic and
interpersonal

Level
upper intermediate

Time
30 minutes

Preparation
one photocopy of
activity sheets A and B
for each student

Extra notes
It would be a good
idea to have coloured
pencils/pens available
for this activity.

Warm-up

❶ Ask the students if they have attended any big music events. Elicit words such as *concert, festival, carnival.* Ask if they enjoyed it and why.

❷ Ask what makes such an event successful. Elicit ideas about the music itself, but also the food, location etc.

Main activity

❶ Give each student activity sheet A. Tell students to read the descriptions of events, then discuss with a partner which one they would like to attend and why.

❷ Tell students they are going to plan their own music event in groups. Hand out activity sheet B and go through it as a class to make sure students understand everything.

❸ Ask students to work individually and complete the first part of the planning sheet with their own ideas. Encourage them to be imaginative.

❹ Put students into groups of four or five and explain that they are now going to share their ideas and come up with a group proposal for a music event.

❺ Explain that they will have to make suggestions and negotiate with each other. Refer them to the expressions in the speech bubbles and check that students undertand them.

❻ Students work in their groups to plan their music event.

❼ When they have finished, each group could present its event to the class.

Follow-up

○ In their groups, ask students to design a poster for their event which includes all the key information about the event, e.g. the type of music, the price of tickets etc.

○ Students could also write a short paragraph advertising their event.

A

Glastonbury Festival

Glastonbury Festival, in England, is an annual event featuring a huge array of music from rock to rap as well as comedy and cabaret performances. The aim of Glastonbury has always been to promote exciting new bands. It is held at Worthy Farm, near Glastonbury, which unfortunately means that most years fans are knee-deep in mud. This is not much fun when they are camping! Fans often bring their own food, but there are many stalls where they can buy food, drinks and even Wellington boots!

Notting Hill Carnival

Notting Hill Carnival is a street carnival held every year in Notting Hill, in London. It goes on for three days and features a huge musical parade through the streets, with amazing floats and hundreds of people in brightly coloured costumes. Originally organised by the Caribbean community in London, it still retains a strong Caribbean flavour. There are traditional steel bands, and much of the music has a Caribbean sound. But the carnival now also aims to celebrate music and cultures from all over the world. This is very obvious in the food stalls along the carnival route, where you can buy exotic food from all over the world.

Charity rock concert

The link between rock music and charity began in 1985, with the huge Live Aid concert which raised money to help starving people in Africa. Since then, there have been many big charity concerts, at which internationally famous bands and musicians have given their time freely to make a difference in the world. The Live 8 concert in 2005 had the slogan 'Make Poverty History' and again raised millions of pounds to help the world's poor. For many people, these concerts represent what is best about the music industry.

B

We could …

What about …?

Why don't we …?

It would be great if …

I'd prefer to …

	My ideas	Group decision
Type of event		
Use of profits		
Location		
Types of music		
Artists		
Other entertainment		
Catering for audience		
Price of tickets		